Equality and Partiality

Equality and Partiality

THOMAS NAGEL

New York   Oxford
OXFORD UNIVERSITY PRESS
1991

Oxford University Press

Oxford   New York   Toronto
Delhi   Bombay   Calcutta   Madras   Karachi
Petaling Jaya   Singapore   Hong Kong   Tokyo
Nairobi   Dar es Salaam   Cape Town
Melbourne   Auckland

and associated companies in
Berlin   Ibadan

Copyright © 1991 by Thomas Nagel

Published by Oxford University Press, Inc.
200 Madison Avenue, New York, NY 10016

Oxford is a registered trademark of Oxford University Press

Library of Congress Cataloging-in-Publication Data

Nagel, Thomas.
Equality and partiality / by Thomas Nagel.
p.   cm.   Includes index.
ISBN 0–19–506967–6
1. Equality.   2. Justice.   I Title
JC575.N25   1991
320'.01'1—dc20   90–19428

9 8 7 6 5 4 3 2 1

Printed in the United States of America
on acid-free paper

To John Rawls
who changed the subject

Acknowledgments

This book was written between 1987 and 1990, and I would like to acknowledge the generous support during that period of the Filomen D'Agostino and Max E. Greenberg Faculty Research Fund of New York University Law School. Some of the material was presented as the Thalheimer Lectures at Johns Hopkins in 1989, and the bulk of it was presented as the John Locke Lectures at Oxford in 1990. An earlier version of Chapter 3 appeared as "What Makes a Political Theory Utopian?" in *Social Research* 56 (1989), and Chapter 14 derives in part from "Moral Conflict and Political Legitimacy," *Philosophy & Public Affairs* 16 (1987).

The book is the result of, and a contribution to, a continuing discussion of moral and political theory with a group of friends and colleagues. I presented the work as it developed to the Colloquium in Law, Philosophy, and Political Theory, conducted jointly every autumn at N.Y.U. Law School by Ronald Dworkin, David Richards, Lawrence Sager, and myself; I benefited greatly from the reactions of those colleagues and of other regular participants, especially Frances Myrna Kamm. I have discussed these subjects over the years, both in conversation and in writing, with T. M. Scanlon, Derek Parfit, and John Rawls, each of whom has had a great and evident influence on my thoughts. In the case of Rawls, the influence now extends over most of my life—since I was a student in his introductory philosophy class at Cornell, one of whose texts was Hobbes's *De Cive*.

In the spring of 1990, when I delivered the John Locke Lectures, I was fortunate enough also to spend two terms at All Souls College as a Visiting Fellow, at a time when there was in

Oxford a particularly happy conjunction of moral and political philosophers to talk to. G. A. Cohen, Ronald Dworkin, Derek Parfit, T. M. Scanlon, Samuel Scheffler, and I met for weekly discussions of our work in progress; we were all working on related problems, and those discussions were wonderfully helpful when I wrote the final draft of the book.

New York   T. N.
January 1991

Contents

Equality and Partiality

1

Introduction

This essay deals with what I believe to be the central problem of political theory. Rather than proposing a solution to it, I shall try to explain what it is, and why a solution is so difficult to achieve. This result need not be thought of pessimistically, since the recognition of a serious obstacle is always a necessary condition of progress, and I believe there is hope that in the future, political and social institutions may develop which continue our unsteady progress toward moral equality, without ignoring the stubborn realities of human nature.

My belief is not just that all social and political arrangements so far devised are unsatisfactory. That might be due to the failure of all actual systems to realize an ideal that we should all recognize as correct. But there is a deeper problem—not merely practical, but theoretical: We do not yet possess an acceptable political ideal, for reasons which belong to moral and political philosophy. The unsolved problem is the familiar one of reconciling the standpoint of the collectivity with the standpoint of the individual; but I want to approach it not primarily as a question about the relation between the individual and society, but in essence and origin as a question about each individual's relation to himself. This reflects a conviction that ethics, and the ethical basis of political theory, have to be understood as arising from a division in each individual between two standpoints, the personal and the impersonal. The latter represents the claims of the collectivity and gives them their force for each individual. If it did not exist, there would be no morality, only the clash, compromise, and occasional convergence of individual perspectives. It is because a human being does not occupy only his own point of view that each of us is susceptible to the claims of others through private and public morality.

Any social arrangement governing the relations among individuals, or between the individual and the collective, depends on a corresponding balance of forces within the self—its image in microcosm. That image is the relation, for each individual, between the personal and impersonal standpoints, on which the social arrangement depends and which it requires of us. If an arrangement is to claim the support of those living under it— if it is to claim legitimacy, in other words—then it must rely on or call into existence some form of reasonable integration of the elements of their naturally divided selves. The division is rough, and spans a great deal of subordinate complexity, but I believe it is indispensable in thinking about the subject.

The hardest problems of political theory are conflicts within the individual, and no external solution will be adequate which does not deal with them at their source. The impersonal standpoint in each of us produces, I shall claim, a powerful demand for universal impartiality and equality, while the personal standpoint gives rise to individualistic motives and requirements which present obstacles to the pursuit and realization of such ideals. The recognition that this is true of everyone then presents the impersonal standpoint with further questions about what is required to treat such persons with equal regard, and this in turn presents the individual with further conflict.

The same problems arise with respect to the morality of personal conduct, but I shall argue that their treatment must be extended to political theory, where the relations of mutual support or conflict between political institutions and individual motivation are all-important. It emerges that a harmonious combination of an acceptable political ideal and acceptable standards of personal morality is very hard to come by. Another way of putting the problem, therefore, is this: When we try to discover reasonable moral standards for the conduct of individuals and then try to integrate them with fair standards for the assessment of social and political institutions, there seems no satisfactory way of fitting the two together. They respond to opposing pressures which cause them to break apart.

To a considerable extent, political institutions and their theoretical justifications try to externalize the demands of the impersonal standpoint. But they have to be staffed and supported and brought to life by individuals for whom the impersonal standpoint coexists with the personal, and this has to be reflected in their design. My claim is that the problem of designing institutions that do justice to the equal importance of all persons, without making unacceptable demands on individuals, has not been solved—and that this is so partly because for our world the problem of the right relation between the personal and impersonal standpoints within each individual has not been solved.

Most people feel this on reflection. We live in a world of spiritually sickening economic and social inequality, a world whose progress toward the acknowledgment of common standards of toleration, individual liberty and human development has been depressingly slow and unsteady. There are sometimes dramatic improvements, and recent events in Eastern Europe must give pause to all those, like myself, who in response to the dominant events of this century have cultivated a defensive pessimism about the prospects of humanity. But we really do not know how to live together. The professed willingness of civilized persons to slaughter each other by the millions in a nuclear war now appears to be subsiding, as the conflicts of political conviction which fueled it lose their sharpness. But even in the developed world, and certainly in the world taken as a whole, the problems which generated the great political and moral rift between democratic capitalism and authoritarian communism have not been solved by the utter competitive failure of the latter.

Communism may have been defeated in Europe, and we may live to celebrate its fall in Asia as well, but that does not mean that democratic capitalism is the last word in human social arrangements. At this historical moment it is worth remembering that communism owes its existence in part to an ideal of equality which remains appealing however great the crimes committed and the economic disasters produced in its name. Democratic societies have not found a way to contend with that ideal: it is a problem for the old democracies of the West, and it will be a very serious problem for the emerging democracies which succeed the collapse of communism in Eastern Europe, and perhaps elsewhere. Political philosophy is not going to transform this situation, but it has its role, for some of the apparently practical problems of political life have theoretical and moral sources. Moral convictions drive political choices, and the absence of moral agreement, if severe, can be far more divisive than a mere conflict of interests. Anyone who is inclined to doubt the connection of political theory with reality cannot hold out against the events now unfolding: moral and theoretical battles are being fought across the globe, sometimes with real tanks.

One should think of political theory as an enterprise of discovery—the discovery of human possibilities whose coming to actuality is encouraged and assisted by the discovery itself. That is certainly how most of the traditional figures of political theory have seen it. They were in the business of imagining the moral future, with the hope of contributing to its realization. But this inevitably carries the risk of utopianism, and that problem is an important aspect of our subject.

A theory is utopian in the pejorative sense if it describes a form of collective life that humans, or most humans, could not lead and could not come to be able to lead through any feasible process of social and mental development. It may have value as a possibility for a few people, or as an admirable but unattainable ideal for others. But it cannot be offered as a general solution to the main question of political theory: How should we live together in society?

Worse still, when what is described is not in fact motivationally possible, the illusion of its possibility may motivate people nevertheless to try to institute it, with results that are quite different. Societies are constantly trying to beat people into shape because they stubbornly fail to conform to some preconceived pattern of human possibility. Political theory is in this sense an empirical discipline whose hypotheses give hostages to the future, and whose experiments can be very costly.[1]

But while the avoidance of utopianism is important, it is no more important than the avoidance of hard-nosed realism, its diametrical opposite. To be sure, a theory that offers new possibilities must be aware of the danger that they may be purely imaginary. The real nature of humans and human motivation always has to be an essential part of the subject: Pessimism is always in order, and we have been given ample reason to fear human nature. But we shouldn't be too tied down by limits derived from the baseness of actual motives or by excessive pessimism about the possibility of human improvement. It is important to try to imagine the next step, even before we have come close to implementing the best conceptions already available.

In this enterprise the use of moral intuition is inevitable, and should not be regretted. To trust our intuitions, particularly those that tell us something is wrong even though we don't know exactly what would be right, we need only believe that our moral understanding extends farther than our capacity to spell out the principles which underlie it. Intuition can be corrupted by custom, self-interest, or commitment to a theory, but it need not be, and often a person's intuitions will provide him with evidence that his own moral theory is missing something, or that the arrangements he has been brought up to find natural are really unjust. Intuitive dissatisfaction is an essential resource in political theory. It can tell us that something is wrong, without necessarily telling us how to fix it. It is a reasonable response to even the most ideal versions of current political practice, and I believe it is the correct response also at the level

1. As Hannah Arendt once said, "It is true that you can't make an omelet without breaking eggs; but you can break a great many eggs without making an omelet."

of theory: It tells us, not surprisingly, that we have not yet arrived at the truth. In that way it can help us to cultivate a healthy dissatisfaction with the familiar, without falling into utopianism of the uncritical sort.

I believe that the clash of personal and impersonal standpoints is one of the most pressing problems revealed in this way. If we cannot, through moral theory and institutional design, reconcile an impartial concern for everyone with a view of how each individual can reasonably be expected to live, then we cannot hope to defend the general acceptability of any political order. These problems of integration come with our humanity, and we cannot expect them ever to disappear. But the attempt to deal with them has to be part of any political theory that can claim to be realistic.

What makes this task so difficult is that our ultimate aim in political theory should be to approach as nearly as possible to unanimity, at some level, in support of the basic framework of those political institutions which are maintained by force and into which we are born. Such a claim may seem extravagant or unintelligible, since lack of unanimity is the essence of politics; but I shall try to defend it, and to explain how it is related to Kantian ethics and to the hypothetical contractualism which is its political expression.

The pure ideal of political legitimacy is that the use of state power should be capable of being *authorized* by each citizen—not in direct detail but through acceptance of the principles, institutions, and procedures which determine how that power will be used. This requires the possibility of unanimous agreement at some sufficiently high level, for if there are citizens who can legitimately object to the way state power is used against them or in their name, the state is not legitimate. To accept such unanimity as an ideal while respecting the complex realities of human motivation and practical reason is inevitably frustrating, but in my conception that is what presents political theory with its task. We must try both to give the condition a morally sensible interpretation and to see how far actual institutions might go toward meeting it.

It is a task which cannot be postponed till the millenium, when conflicts have disappeared and all share a common goal. The secular form of that seductive and dangerous vision, which condemns the aim of even idealized agreement under existing circumstances, and insists on struggle and the pursuit of victory so long as there are classes whose interests conflict, has been Marx's most conspicuous moral legacy to the world. Harmony is reserved for a future which will be achieved only by eschewing harmony for political war between irreconcilable interests in the present.

This view should be rejected, and the pursuit of human equality decisively separated from it. The aim of idealized agreement has a role at all stages in the pursuit of an improved human condition, even if full justice is far away. Force will always be necessary if that aim is not widely enough shared, but it is a disaster to exclude the aim from political morality until history has proceeded by other means to that mythical terminus at which it will be effortlessly achieved.

2

Two Standpoints

Most of our experience of the world, and most of our desires, belong to our individual points of view: We see things *from here*, so to speak. But we are also able to think about the world in abstraction from our particular position in it—in abstraction from who we are. It is possible to abstract much more radically than that from the contingencies of the self. For example, in pursuit of the kind of objectivity needed in the physical sciences, we abstract even from our humanity. But nothing further than abstraction from our identity (that is, *who* we are) enters into ethical theory.[2] Each of us begins with a set of concerns, desires, and interests of his own, and each of us can recognize that the same is true of others. We can then remove ourselves in thought from our particular position in the world and think simply of all those people, without singling out as *I* the one we happen to be.

By performing this deed of abstraction we occupy what I shall call the impersonal standpoint. From that position, the content and character of the different individual standpoints one can survey remain unchanged: One has set aside only the fact that a particular standpoint is one's own, if any of them is. It isn't that one doesn't know; one just omits this fact from the description of the situation.

A great deal emerges from our capacity to view the world in this way, including the great enterprise of trying to discover the objective nature of reality. But since objectivity also has its sig-

2. I have discussed the wider topic in *The View From Nowhere*.

nificance with respect to values and the justification of conduct, the impersonal standpoint plays an essential role in the evaluation of political institutions. Ethics and political theory begin when from the impersonal standpoint we focus on the raw data provided by the individual desires, interests, projects, attachments, allegiances and plans of life that define the personal points of view of the multitude of distinct individuals, ourselves included. What happens at that point is that we recognize some of these things to have impersonal value. Things do not simply cease to matter when viewed impersonally, and we are forced to recognize that they matter not only *to* particular individuals or groups.

I have argued before, and I continue to believe, that it is impossible to avoid this consequence if one juxtaposes personal and impersonal standpoints toward one's own life. You cannot sustain an impersonal indifference to the things in your life which matter to you personally: some of the most important have to be regarded as mattering, period, so that others besides yourself have reason to take them into account. But since the impersonal standpoint does not single you out from anyone else, the same must be true of the values arising in other lives. If you matter impersonally so does everyone.

We can usefully think of the values that go into the construction of a political theory as being revealed in a series of four stages, each of which depends on a moral response to an issue posed by what was revealed at the previous stage. At the first stage, the basic insight that appears from the impersonal standpoint is that everyone's life matters, and no one is more important than anyone else. This does not mean that some people may not be more important in virtue of their greater value for others. But at the baseline of value in the lives of individuals, from which all higher-order inequalities of value must derive, everyone counts the same. For a given quantity of whatever it is that's good or bad—suffering or happiness or fulfillment or frustration—its intrinsic impersonal value doesn't depend on whose it is.

There are so many people one can barely imagine it, and

their aims and interests interfere with one another; but what happens to each of them is enormously important—as important as what happens to you. The importance of their lives to them, if we really take it in, ought to be reflected in the importance their lives are perceived to have from the impersonal standpoint, even if not all elements of those lives will be accorded an impersonal value corresponding to its personal value to the individual whose life it is—a qualification I leave aside for the moment.

Given this enormous multitude of things that matter impersonally, values positive and negative pointing in every conceivable direction, the problem for the impersonal standpoint is to determine how the elements should be combined and conflicts among them resolved, so that we can evaluate alternatives that affect different individuals differently in ways that matter to them.

The response to this problem is the second stage in the generation of ethics from its raw material in personal value. I won't try to defend even a partial solution yet, but my belief is that the right form of impersonal regard for everyone is an impartiality among individuals that is egalitarian not merely in the sense that it counts them all the same as inputs to some combinatorial function, but in the sense that the function itself gives preferential weight to improvements in the lives of those who are worse off as against adding to the advantages of those better off—though all improvements will count positively to some degree. This is obviously related to the egalitarian element in Rawls's theory of social justice, but I believe something of the kind is true in ethics more generally. I believe also that the degree of preference to the worst off depends not just on their position relative to the better off, but also on how badly off they are, absolutely. Alleviation of urgent needs and serious deprivation has particularly strong importance in the acceptable resolution of conflicts of interest.[3]

3. See David Wiggins, "Claims of Need."

We are talking now about how things appear from an entirely impersonal standpoint, one it would be natural to take up if we were looking from outside at a situation to which we were personally unconnected. The point is that we can also adopt this stance by abstraction toward situations in which we are involved, either personally or by connection with someone else. If we ask ourselves, considering all the lives affected, what would be best, or how to determine which of several alternatives would be better, we are pulled toward the conclusion that what happens to anyone matters the same as if it had happened to anyone else, that the elimination of the worst sufferings and deprivations matters most, that improvements at higher levels matter gradually less, and that at roughly equivalent levels of well-being, larger quantities of improvement or the reverse and larger numbers of individuals matter more.[4]

This is at least consistent with some familiar moral feelings. When we survey the actual world from the impersonal standpoint, its sufferings press in upon us: The alleviation of misery, ignorance, and powerlessness, and the elevation of most of our fellow human beings to a minimally decent standard of existence, seem overwhelmingly important, and the first requirement of any social or political arrangement would seem to be its likelihood of contributing to this goal. That is the clear impersonal judgment as to what matters most—the judgment one would make if one were observing the world from outside. And if one were actually a powerful and benevolent outsider, dispensing benefits to the inhabitants of the world, one would probably try to produce the best result by the impartial and egalitarian measure I have sketched.

However, the story does not stop here, because neither ethics nor political theory have as their aim to provide advice to a

---

4. This means that we can make evaluative comparisons among alternatives that are better for some individuals and worse for others. Two different Pareto-optimal arrangements may be compared, and one found to be better, even though each of them is worse for somebody: The better alternative need not be better or at least as good for everybody.

outside them all—as happens in the attitude of pure impartial benevolence. But perhaps I can refer to it instead as the Kantian development of the impersonal standpoint.

What the impersonal standpoint generates at the first and second stages is a massive impartial addition to each individual's values without any indication of how this is to be combined with the personal values that were already there. The individual is of course counted as one among the many whose life is seen to have value from the impersonal standpoint, but that does not make his special personal interest in his own life go away. This is, I think, an acutely uncomfortable position. There is no obvious way of doing justice to the demands of both these perspectives at the same time—for example, by construing them as subordinate aspects of a single, higher-order evaluative system. Yet fulfillment of the one will almost inevitably clash with fulfillment of the other. That may be true even of the worst off who are most favored by an egalitarian impartiality, since their individual interests may not correspond to what would serve the interests of their fellows. So each of us, after the results of the first stage of impersonal evaluation have been assimilated, is likely to find himself severely torn.

The question is, how can we put ourselves back together? The political problem, as Plato believed, must be solved within the individual soul if it is to be solved at all. This does not mean that the solution will not deal with interpersonal relations and public institutions. But it means that such "external" solutions will be valid only if they give expression to an adequate response to the division of the self, conceived as a problem for each individual.

Something more than the original attitude of impartiality will be required to deal with this issue, even when we think of it from the impersonal standpoint. Impartiality alone could only add the anxieties of inner conflict to the set of human ills, and include their reduction among its aims for everyone. But this would leave the problem essentially unchanged for particular individuals whose more personal aims conflicted with the collective good thus redefined. What is needed instead is some general method of resolving the inner conflict that can be applied universally and that is acceptable to everyone in light of the universality of that conflict. But here the values universally recognized will have a different form, specifying what in light of the full complement of factors it is reasonable for each person to do and want, rather than what results are better or worse. The idea of what is reasonable, which will play a significant part in this discussion, is the object of a Kantian judgment: It is what I can affirm that anyone ought to do in my place, and what therefore everyone ought to agree that it is right for me to do as things are.

Whether this is a well-defined idea is a notoriously difficult question, familiar to anyone who has tried to interpret the categorical imperative. The solution to this problem, if there is one, would constitute the third stage in the progression from the personal to the ethical.

The problem of integration has to be approached both through the morality of individual conduct and through the design of those institutions, conventions, and rules in which it is embedded. We must ask not only what type and degree of contribution to impersonal aims can reasonably be asked of divided creatures like ourselves, but also how we or our circumstances might reasonably hope to be transformed so that a life which better meets both sets of demands would become possible for us. This shows the connection between the ethics of individual conduct and political theory, and brings us finally to the fourth stage in the generation of ethics.

Political institutions can be regarded as in part the response to an ethical demand: the demand for creation of a context in which it will be possible for each of us to live a decent and integrated life, both because the effects of our actions are altered by the context and because we ourselves are transformed by our place in it. Political institutions serve some of the same purposes as moral conventions, though our participation in them, unlike obedience to moral requirements, is not voluntary but coercively imposed. This together with their much greater complexity and role differentiation gives them exceptional powers of transformation, for better or for worse.

The contents of the personal standpoint can be altered not only by changes in the structure of incentives but by changes in the sense of who we are, what our ends are, and where our personal fulfillment is to be found. But it is perfectly clear, as a psychological matter, that the special concern with how one's own life goes cannot be abolished or even, except in unusual cases, minimized. However powerful the impartial, egalitarian values of the impersonal standpoint may be, they have to be realized by institutions and systems of conduct that face up to the irreducibility of the individual point of view which is always present alongside the impersonal standpoint, however highly developed the latter may be. The individual point of view is not only a perspective on the facts and a causal point of contact—essential of course for acting within the world—but a perspective of value. It can distort the perception of impersonal values, but even if it does not, it provides its own, independent version of what matters to each of us.

The ideal, then, is a set of institutions within which persons can live a collective life that meets the impartial requirements of the impersonal standpoint while at the same time having to conduct themselves only in ways that it is reasonable to require of individuals with strong personal motives. But to state this ideal is to see how hard it will be to realize. Its two conditions pull in contrary directions.

The conflict between personal and impersonal standpoints is particularly conspicuous for those who are relatively fortunate, but it forces itself also on the unfortunate, not only through possible opposition between their concern for themselves and the equal claims of others like them, but through the issue of how much they may legitimately ask of others who are better off. At some point the natural demand for egalitarian impartiality has to come to terms with a recognition that legitimate claims of personal life exist even for those who are not in need.

But let me add immediately that we are nowhere near that point. In the grossly unequal world in which we live, the primary significance of the impersonal standpoint for those at the bottom of the social heap is that it compounds their personal wretchedness with a perception that they do not really count in the eyes of the world. To suffer from the unavoidable blows of fate is bad enough; to suffer because others do not accord one's life its true value is worse. We would have to move a considerable distance toward improvement in the condition of most human lives before the claims of the better off presented a serious challenge to the pursuit of further equality at their expense.

There may be those who think that I have exaggerated the problem by exaggerating the strength of the values perceived in the first instance from the impersonal standpoint. Does everyone really matter that much from a detached perspective? There is a genuine philosophical problem here. A skeptic might hold that *nothing* matters from the impersonal standpoint—that all that matters is what matters to this or that individual. I believe as already indicated that this is untenable, but won't try to argue further against it here.[5] More to the point, I believe that if people's lives matter impersonally at all, they matter hugely. They matter so much, in fact, that the recognition of it is hard to bear, and most of us engage in some degree of suppression of the impersonal standpoint in order to avoid facing our pathetic failure to meet its claims.

If the suppression is sufficiently effective, it may give currency to the idea that political theory ought really to concern itself only with the accommodation of individual interests, among parties each of whom cares only about himself and a few other people. But I believe that any political theory that merits respect has to offer us an escape from the self-protective blocking out of the importance of others, which we may find psychologically unavoidable in a badly arranged world but which involves the denial of an essential aspect of ourselves. Suppression of

5. The possibility is discussed in *The View From Nowhere*, chaps. 8 and 11.

the full force of the impersonal standpoint is denial of our full humanity, and of the basis for a full recognition of the value of our own lives. That is a loss which all of us should want to escape, even if it has to some extent the effect of concealing from us its own cost.

Everyone has reasons deriving from the impersonal standpoint to want the world to be arranged in a way that accords better with the demands of impartiality—whatever may be the relation of such a development to his personal interests. Any political theory that aspires to moral decency must try to devise and justify a form of institutional life which answers to the real strength of impersonal values while recognizing that that is not all we have to reckon with. Any moral theory which is not related to such a political theory must be regarded as incomplete.

3

The Problem of Utopianism

The duality of standpoints makes its appearance in political theory with particular prominence as the root of an old and persistent problem—the problem of utopianism.

Political theory typically has both an ideal and a persuasive function. It presents an ideal of collective life, and it tries to show people one by one that they should want to live under it. These ambitions may be universal, or they may be more local, but in either case there is a serious question of how they can be realized jointly, and whether they necessarily interfere with one another. An ideal, however attractive it may be to contemplate, is utopian if reasonable individuals cannot be motivated to live by it. But a political system that is completely tied down to individual motives may fail to embody any ideal at all.

One might try to subordinate the persuasive to the ideal function by saying that a political theory should concern itself exclusively with what is right, for if it can be shown that a certain form of social organization is the right one, that should be all the reason anyone needs to want it to be realized. But this seems excessively high-minded, and it ignores the relevance of what is motivationally reasonable to what is right. If real people find it psychologically very difficult or even impossible to live as the theory requires, or to adopt the relevant institutions, that should carry some weight against the ideal.

On the other hand, this accommodation has its own problems: One has to be careful not to turn it into an excuse for giving up too easily; there is a danger that one will get into the

support. This sort of legitimacy is the ambition of thinkers as widely separated in their assumptions about human nature as Hobbes and Rousseau.

The existence of some kind of truth and the possibility of justification to all are bound together here in a way that forces us to wonder whether human beings have enough in common, despite their conflicts, to permit a political argument to be addressed to them all. This brings us back to the duality of standpoints. The danger of utopianism comes from the political tendency, in pursuit of the ideal of moral equality, to put too much pressure on individual motives or even to attempt to transcend them entirely through an impersonal transformation of social individuals. A nonutopian solution requires a proper balance between these elements, and that requires knowing what they are and how they interact.

A particularly important aspect of the search for an unforced solution is the discovery of conditions which permit a peaceful division of authority between the two standpoints. An individual can be moved simultaneously by personal motives having to do with his particular life and particular concerns, and by impersonal motives which are impartial among all persons—himself, his friends, and total strangers. These sets of motives coexist, but they need not compete directly in every choice or decision. Sometimes there is a division of motivational authority.

For example, if you and I discover that we both want the last eclair on the dessert tray, we won't engage in a shoving match but will probably let the result be determined by a mutually acceptable even if arbitrary procedure, or give the preference to the one who was there first, if that can be determined. In doing this, neither of us has to give up his personal preference that he should be the one to get the eclair. We just inhibit its motivational effect for the time being, and shift to an impartial gear in order to settle the matter.

Unfortunately this may not always be possible. If each of us wants the last life jacket for his child as the ship goes down, we may not be able to switch off the effects of this personal motive in favor of an impartial procedure, simply because the personal motive is overwhelming. And in some ethical theories this would be counted not as a moral failure, but as an inevitable limit on the claims of impartiality and equality within morality. But though there are limits, civilized life consists in a constant overlap of impersonally supported practices and individual aims, with the impersonal requiring us to restrict or inhibit the pursuit of the personal without giving it up. To be socialized is to contain these different points of view in some kind of internal harmony.

I believe that some accommodation of this kind is itself part of the morality of individual conduct, rather than the result of a conflict between self-interest and morality, or an exemption of individuals from moral requirements. Morality allows compartments for individual pursuits, while defining their boundaries by general standards.

The problem of compartmentalization and its limits is central to political theory, which differs from ethical theory in arguing not just for certain forms of voluntary conduct, but for acceptance of the authority of institutions over which the individual may have little personal control, and which may do things in his name or to him that he would not have chosen, even if he had stuck to his ethical principles. Subjecting oneself to external force carries rather different risks from committing oneself to a principle of personal conduct. Individual morality may offer the individual less protection than political institutions do, but political institutions create a larger potential threat to the individual, in virtue of the same power that offers him greater protection. He cannot opt out if the costs get too high.

Political institutions sometimes serve all our interests more or less equally. But they may also serve the interests of some much more than others, or may actually sacrifice the interests of some to others. To justify a choice among the alternatives to everyone it is necessary to identify both the claims of impartiality or moral equality and the claims of individual motivation, and find an arrangement which appeals to them in a feasible combination.

But what is the standard of feasibility? It is not clear how one can allow supposed psychological facts about natural human resistance to impartiality to determine the conditions of moral justification, without being guilty of capitulation to simple human *badness*. What is the proper relation between motivation and justification in ethical or political theory? The answer is that political theory must take into account the individual conduct it demands of people in the creation and operation of political institutions, and the character of the motivation required for that conduct, but that the evaluation of these individual implications is not merely political, nor merely psychological, but ethical. It is necessary to consider what reasons—moral and other—individuals may have for and against acting in the necessary ways, and what kinds of lives will result from the combined effects of those motives.

The process of evaluation is complicated, because the motives are not independent of political and ethical theory. Ethical argument reveals possibilities of moral motivation that cannot be understood without it, and in political theory these possibilities are elaborated through institutions to which people are able to adhere partly because of their moral attractiveness. It may even be possible to alter people's conception of the boundary between personal and impersonal values by means of conventions or institutions which extend the scope of the public domain, and change the forms which individual autonomy can take. But people are motivationally complex, and a moral argument cannot transform them into beings of a completely different kind. Neither can a revolutionary new political arrangement. What is right must be possible, even if our understanding of what is possible can be partly transformed by arguments about what is right.

This doesn't mean that we are not justified in taking political steps which substantial numbers of people will be unable to accept. To abolish a fundamental injustice such as slavery, serfdom, a caste system, or the subjugation of women, it is usually necessary to impose large losses on those who may regard themselves as entitled to its benefits. But the idea in such cases is that when we come through to the other side of the transformation, perhaps only after a generation or two, the resulting arrangement will command the acceptance, out of a mixture of impartial and personal motives, of a much wider range of persons than the old arrangement did—that it will prove a viable and superior form of collective life.

A project of transformation is often condemned as utopian if it will not lead to a result which is stable in this sense—a result which generates its own support by calling forth new possibilities of mutual respect and recognition of moral equality through adherence to cooperative institutions. Moral as well as political viability seems to depend on a relation of mutual support among moral justification, individual motives, and institutional frameworks, rules, or conventions. This goal of moral stability through the mutual reinforcement of just institutions and individual psychology receives prominent expression in Rawls's concept of a well-ordered society. The problem of utopianism can be thought of as the problem of discovering the constraints on a well-ordered society.[6]

Let me illustrate with a negative example. Attempts to create a classless society have spectacularly failed the test of moral transformation so far, and the hope that it can be done is now widely thought of as utopian. This is a particularly conspicuous illustration of the way in which political theory is hostage to human nature. It is no use to assert that we all ought to be working for the common good and that this requires the abolition of private property in the means of production. If the personal element of most people's motivation cannot be shrunk enough or the impersonal element expanded enough, a system of comprehensive public ownership seems doomed to degenerate under a combination of stagnation, nepotism, and a par-

6. See John Rawls, *A Theory of Justice*, pp. 453–62.

allel black market, not to mention the political oppression and cruelty which may be required to keep it in place. Perhaps the possibilities of much greater equality are there, but so far radical institutions have failed to evoke them: Altruism appears to be just as scarce in socialist as in capitalist societies, and the employment of strong-arm methods to make up the deficit has not been a success.

Some of the problems can be attributed to the specific character of twentieth-century communism, which was probably worse than it had to be. And there is no way to rule out in advance the possibility that alternative arrangements might some day be devised which would prevent the development of socioeconomic classes without tyranny and without requiring a fundamental transformation of personal motives. At this point, however, such a possibility is completely abstract. As things are, a decent classless society seems unachievable.

Yet class stratification is clearly an evil: How could it not be an evil that some people's life prospects at birth are radically inferior to others'? And it is not like the evil that some people are born with congenital handicaps: The remedy seems at least conceivable in a different set of social arrangements, fueled by different motives. Even if a market is needed for the efficient interaction of supply and demand, it is not beyond imagination that some incentive other than personal gain might drive the minimization of costs and the maximization of profits. Yet most people are not in fact adequately motivated to make such arrangements work, and will tend to try to circumvent them if they are forcibly imposed. So an initially attractive moral ideal is blocked by a recalcitrant human nature: Does this reveal the sinful inadequacy of human beings or the utopian inadequacy of communism?

I dwell on this example not only because of its currency in our time but because it exemplifies the central features of the problem we are discussing:

1. Impersonally considered, the ideal of eliminating inherited economic inequality is morally attractive.

2. The institutions and patterns of voluntary behavior needed to realize this ideal seem *conceivable*, at least in outline. (I realize that this is speculative.)

3. There is considerable evidence from people's actual behavior under a variety of institutions that they have powerful personal motives, impossible to eradicate, which lead them to behave differently.

4. The maintenance of such a system in the face of these motives seems to require pervasive governmental control of individual life, serious denials of liberty, strict enforcement of general ignorance, and the absence of democracy. Even then it doesn't achieve an egalitarian result, since those in control of the system manipulate it to their own advantage.

5. Finally, if people could become different so that they would support a thriving system of economic equality freely, they would thereby become not worse as individuals, but in some ways better. They would not have to submerge all their personal motives and concerns beneath a desire for the common good, but need only (only!) give up their acquisitiveness and greatly expand their public-spiritedness and devotion to productive labor for its own sake.

Such a change in most people's character is hard to imagine, except perhaps through the effect over many generations of social institutions that have not been invented yet. This conflict between impersonal ideals and individual motivation reflects the basic division within individuals that we have already discussed. It is possible for individuals to judge from an impersonal standpoint that a certain form of collective conduct or a certain set of interpersonal relations would be good—or better than what we have now—without being thereby sufficiently motivated to do what would be necessary to play their part in such an arrangement.

There are several different problems of reconciling what is collectively desirable with what is individually reasonable, and I am not concerned with all of them. The most familiar is a co-

ordination problem: Each of us may want a certain result which
depends on the cooperation of others, but each may be insufficiently motivated to cooperate unless he can be assured that
the others will too. Another, more acute form is the Prisoners'
Dilemma: Each of us may want a result which depends on the
cooperation of all, but each may be insufficiently motivated to
cooperate *whether the others do or whether they don't*. These problems can arise even where we are dealing only with a single
motive—self-interest, for example—which simultaneously leads
us to desire the cooperative solution and motivates us not to
play our individual part in it.

Such problems, and their solutions, are very important for
political theory. But I am particularly concerned with the type
of case in which *different* motives enter at the level of individual
choice to prevent realization of what is impersonally desired.
(Of course these distinct types of conflict can be present simultaneously.) When one descends from the level of impersonal
assessment to contemplate playing one's role in a social institution, the claims of individual life and personal projects and
commitments assert themselves. The impersonal desires are not
left behind, but there is a lot more to each of us than what goes
into the formation of such desires, and what it is reasonable for
us to *do* depends on the full range of reasons operating in our
lives.

The central point is this. Justification in political theory must
address itself to people twice: first as occupants of the impersonal standpoint and second as occupants of particular roles
within an impersonally acceptable system. This is not capitulation to human badness or weakness, but a necessary acknowledgment of human complexity. To ignore the second task is to
risk utopianism in the bad sense. And to attempt it is not to
abandon the primacy of moral justification in political theory,
but simply to recognize that personal as well as impersonal justification has a part in morality. The requirement of dual justification is a moral requirement.

The difficulty is to explain the difference between legitimate consideration for individual points of view and moral sponginess. Somehow the standards for justification to individuals either in ethics generally or in political theory should emerge from an assessment of the importance of personal motives which has general validity and can therefore be impersonally acknowledged: What is reasonable in personal motivation is itself the object of a general ethical judgment.

An individual considering the weight to be accorded to personal motives in general should not allow his judgment to be influenced by those personal motives which are specifically present in him—though he will be influenced by the recognition of the force and importance of those motives for anyone, himself included. He may be legitimately influenced in his conduct by those motives, but only in ways that he must acknowledge would be legitimate for anyone. The question is not just what is practically feasible, but what is justifiable. An acceptable answer, though it is influenced by a recognition of the importance of individual motives, must be impersonally and universally acceptable and not just the result of individual resistance to the claims of ethics.

By this standard it seems likely that a regime in which everyone is expected to be driven by impartial benevolence for all other members of the community would fail the test, as would many less ambitious proposals. But there is also a real possibility that no system of social organization yet devised would pass the test, and even that none ever *could* pass it with flying colors. The problem is that since any system must be justified twice, it may be impossible to devise a system which is acceptable both from the point of view of what would be impersonally desirable, and from the point of view of what can reasonably be demanded of individuals—even where that question too is being answered universally, in the Kantian mode. For example, class stratification may be impersonally unacceptable, but so may some of the requirements on individuals imposed by any social institutions we can think of that would eliminate it.

But it is no good to say *either* that people are just bad if they fail to behave individually in the way that would produce an impersonally desirable outcome, *or* that since they can't legitimately be required to behave in that way, the ideal should be given up. Instead we should regard both of the elements that create the dilemma as morally valid; we are then faced with an unsatisfactory situation which calls for the exercise of political, social, and psychological imagination. What generates political theory as a distinct subject is an ethical demand and not just a practical one—and it is the demand for ethical invention rather than merely for the application of individual morality to group conduct. The problem is to increase the degree to which both personal and impersonal values can be harmoniously satisfied in spite of their natural rivalry.

Coercion, assured compliance, and the engagement of individual interests will obviously play a part in any political solution, but they are not sufficient. A fully realized social ideal has to engage the impersonal allegiance of individuals while at the same time permitting their personal motives some free play in the conduct demanded by the system, thus permitting the coexistence and integration of elements in each individual's makeup which are potentially at war with one another. The absence of such a solution produces the bad conscience in civilization with which we are so familiar.

To deal with the problem by attempting to shrink the domain of the private to a tiny compass by an assault on individualism is foolish, and to the extent that it succeeds it will destroy most of what is valuable in human life. Yet something must be done to decrease the disharmony between individual motives and those social ideals that any defender of individualism must recognize. This cannot be achieved entirely by ingenuities of social design, nor simply through a change of heart. To the extent that it is possible at all, it requires a nonutopian development of individual rationality in response to changes in the social medium for its expression.

4

Legitimacy and Unanimity

What we want to avoid is utopianism on the one hand and moral abdication on the other. What we want to achieve is legitimacy. We may think of the problem as that of reinterpreting political legitimacy in light of the complex character of practical reason, in order to see how its conditions might be met.

The task of discovering the conditions of legitimacy is traditionally conceived as that of finding a way to justify a political system to everyone who is required to live under it. If the justification is successful, no one will have grounds for moral complaint about the way it takes into account and weighs his interests and point of view. Even though he might be able to think of alternative arrangements more advantageous to him, still on balance, taking everyone's point of view into account together with his own, no one living under such a system will have grounds for objection to the way it treats him.

This is an ideal. As I have said, the search for legitimacy is a search for unanimity—not about everything but about the controlling framework within which more controversial decisions will be made. The unanimity in question is neither actual unanimity among persons with the motives they happen to have, nor the kind of ideal unanimity that simply follows from there being a single right answer which everyone ought to accept because it is independently right, but rather something in between: a unanimity which could be achieved among persons in many respects as they are, provided they were also reasonable and committed within reason to modifying their claims, requirements, and motives in a direction which makes a common framework of justification possible. This is an application of the Kantian unanimity criterion simultaneously to political institutions and to the individual lives of their members.

If such a hypothetical unanimity were discoverable, it would explain the rightness of the answer rather than being explained by it. That is, it would not be possible to discover what everyone should agree to by a single course of reasoning which everyone can follow to the same result. Rather, the right result would be discoverable only by finding that different persons, reasoning from their different perspectives, will converge on it. This is a tall order on any conception of practical reason. People are different and their interests conflict, so the aim of justification to everyone is very ambitious, even if we are permitted to set the boundaries of the political community so as to maximize the chance of such justification.

It is possible to attempt to carry out the project solely in terms of personal values and motives, as Hobbes did by appealing to each individual's dominant need for security. Hobbes's modern descendants concentrate on finding equilibrium conditions among independent decision-makers, using the methods of game theory.[7] I do not favor this route, since I believe the impersonal standpoint makes an essential contribution to individual motivation which must be addressed by any ethically acceptable theory. For that matter, even theories which direct their justifications exclusively to the personal standpoint need to say something about why legitimacy is desirable, and it is difficult to do this without appealing to impersonal values of some kind—for example the necessity of treating people as ends and not as means merely. Otherwise why should we care about justifying the system to more people than we have to in order to secure stability? If those who can't accept it are a weak enough minority, they can be forcibly kept in line by the rest of us. It would not be plausible to suggest that everyone has a *personal* interest in the

7. See David Gauthier, *Morals by Agreement.*

justifiability of the political order to everyone else—even though Hobbes believed that what justified it to one would in fact justify it to all.

I shall assume, then, that some form of impartiality enters into the pursuit of legitimacy at its foundation. Not only does it motivate that pursuit, but it is one of the motivational resources that has to be appealed to in offering the desired justifications. Because of the character of these justifications, legitimacy is a moral concept. If a system is legitimate, those living under it have no grounds for complaint against the way its basic structure accommodates their point of view, and no one is morally justified in withholding his cooperation from the functioning of the system, trying to subvert its results, or trying to overturn it if he has the power to do so. (This is to be distinguished from trying to do better for oneself within the bounds or under the rules of the system, without challenging its legitimacy.)

An illegitimate system, on the other hand, treats some of those living under it in such a way that they can reasonably feel that their interests and point of view have not been adequately accommodated—so that, even taking into account the interests of others, their own point of view puts them reasonably in opposition to the system. In that case, other things being equal, it would not be wrong for them to withhold their cooperation from it, try to subvert its results, or replace it with one more favorable to their interests if they were able to do so.

Legitimacy is not the same thing as stability. A legitimate system may be unstable because some parties subvert it without justification. An illegitimate system may be stable because, although some parties would be justified in subverting it if they could, they are too weak to do so, or it is in their interest to accept accommodation with others as a modus vivendi, rather than risk conflict or defeat by trying for a preferred alternative. Legitimacy implies that there is no moral justification for disrupting or subverting the system; but even when it would not be morally objectionable to do so, it may be either impossible

or imprudent to try. Flagrantly illegitimate systems can therefore be quite stable.

The search for legitimacy can be thought of as an attempt to
realize some of the values of voluntary participation, in a system of institutions that is unavoidably compulsory. Subjection
to a political system cannot be made voluntary: Even if some
people can leave, that is very difficult or impossible for most of
them. In any case all people are born and spend their forma-
tive years under a system over which they have no control. To
show that they all have sufficient reason to accept it is as close
as we can come to making this involuntary condition voluntary.
We try to show that it would be unreasonable for them to reject
the option of living under such a system, even though the choice
cannot be offered.

In defining legitimacy in this way I have adopted the central
feature of Scanlon's account of contractualism—the idea that
the right principles to govern a practice are those which no one
could reasonably reject, given the aim of finding principles which
could be the basis of general agreement among persons simi-
larly motivated. To quote Scanlon's rule more fully:

> An act is wrong if its performance under the circumstances would
> be disallowed by any system of rules for the regulation of behav-
> iour which no one could reasonably reject as a basis for in-
> formed, unforced general agreement.[8]

He employs the strong condition, "no one could reject"—similar to "everyone must accept"—rather than the weaker "everyone *could* accept." While this makes justification difficult, it seems
the right standard of unanimity to try to meet. The range of
institutions that people *could* accept without being unreasonable
is far too broad—if one is willing to regard substantial levels of
voluntary self-sacrifice as not unreasonable.

Although Scanlon is discussing contractualism as a moral theory, the extension to the conditions of political legitimacy is quite
natural, substituting "enforced conformity" for "unforced gen-

---

8. T. M. Scanlon, "Contractualism and Utilitarianism," p. 110.

eral agreement."[9] The step is not as great as it may seem, in virtue of the ideal of quasi-voluntariness which legitimacy aims at. The idea is that behind the coercion that has an unavoidable role in any political system there should be independent reasons for everyone to cooperate voluntarily in the maintenance of such a system and to respect its results. Coercion is not the basis of a legitimate political system, but merely one feature that plays an instrumental role, however essential, in its operation and the maintenance of its stability—a feature that is warranted only in virtue of the legitimacy of the system which contains it.

Being a hypothetical contractualist position, Scanlon's principle is of course related to Kant's categorical imperative, but it is worth observing just how close the relation is. Consider the class of general rules that no one could reasonably reject. The complement of this class consists of rules that at least one person could reasonably reject. And a rule of this sort is, on a natural interpretation, one that no one could will as a universal law, since it would be unwillable for the case in which he imagines himself in the position of that person. A maxim of which it was the universalization would therefore fail to satisfy the categorical imperative. So allowing for differences, Scanlon's principle and the categorical imperative have the following property in common: A course of action is prohibited by either of them if and only if every universal rule of conduct which would permit it falls within this complementary class of rejectable principles.

What would it mean to claim that something could not reasonably be rejected by individuals with the dual nature I have claimed we all have? Let me first answer this question in abstract terms. Each of us has a primary attachment to his own personal interests, projects, and commitments, but this is restrained by our occupation of the impersonal standpoint in two

---

9. Charles Beitz has applied Scanlon's conception with interesting results to an important issue of political theory in *Political Equality*.

ways: first, by the recognition of the equal objective importance
of what happens to everyone, and second, by the recognition
of the special importance for each person of his own point of
view and the reasonableness of some natural partiality. So we
are simultaneously partial to ourselves, impartial among everyone, and respectful of everyone else's partiality.

When these factors conflict, as they inevitably will, there is
for each person an accommodation of his partiality which is
reasonable in light of the interests and partiality of others. If
he is more partial to himself than this in what he takes or insists
upon, he is being unreasonable. If, on the other hand, an arrangement does not afford him the consideration which it is
reasonable for him to require, in virtue of the partiality toward
himself which is permissible even in light of a due regard for
the interests and partiality of others, then he is not unreasonable to reject it and try to impose an alternative which it *would*
be unreasonable for him to reject.

I have offered no substantive standards for such reasonableness, but have only indicated what factors bear on it in each
individual case. Legitimacy is the result of a convergence from
different perspectives on a single arrangement as satisfying the
conditions of nonrejectability for each of them. (As will be seen,
there is no guarantee that such convergence will be possible—
whether in a given situation an arrangement can be devised
which each individual from his perspective would be unreasonable to reject, going by general standards of reasonableness of
the kind described.)

A legitimate system is one which reconciles the two universal
principles of impartiality and reasonable partiality so that no
one can object that his interests are not being accorded sufficient weight or that the demands made on him are excessive.
What makes it reasonable for someone to reject a system, and
therefore makes it illegitimate, is either that it leaves him too
badly off by comparison with others (which corresponds to a
failure with respect to impartiality), or that it demands too much
of him by way of sacrifice of his interests or commitments by

comparison with some feasible alternative (which corresponds to a failure with respect to reasonable partiality).

Of course what counts as too badly off or too demanding depends on the costs to others, in these same terms, of the alternatives. The reasonableness of a complaint depends on general standards for the accommodation of partiality and impartiality, and anyone else can recognize its validity as well as the person who makes it. Still, there is a correspondence between complaints coming from particular people and certain types of impersonal objections, which reflects the character of legitimacy as a search for unanimity. If someone reasonably rejects a system on the ground that it neglects his needs, or on the ground that it demands too great a sacrifice of his personal projects, he is both appealing to an objective standard and invoking the personal motive that will lead him to resist the system which fails him by that standard.

But this is not a mere threat. What it is reasonable to reject is a moral issue, "all the way down," and not one that is settled by how much this or that party to the arrangement can hold out for in virtue of superior bargaining power. Differences in bargaining power carry no moral weight in themselves, even if they can be given authority to determine results within a system that is legitimate by a standard of acceptability that is not the result of bargaining power.

The question is, what supplies the standard of reasonable, morally permissible rejection which provides the true test of the legitimacy of a system, as opposed to rejection based only on superior leverage and unmodified self-interest? We know that the intrusion of such a nonmoral, baldly political element into the process of justification could be avoided by the elevation of impartiality to a position of complete dominance; but fortunately that is not the only way. While the attitude of impartiality which is the first consequence of the impersonal standpoint will play an important part in determining any acceptable result, it must come to an accommodation with the personal standpoint somehow, by seeking principles that recognize the importance of those aims in each person's life and determine how much weight they must be given in general. To accommodate the personal standpoint within ethics we need a theory of *agent-relative* reasons for action—reasons specified by universal principles which nevertheless refer ineliminably to features or circumstances of the agent for whom they are reasons. The contrast is with *agent-neutral* reasons, which depend on what everyone ought to value, independently of its relation to himself.[10]

The conception of morality which I would defend includes general principles for both agent-neutral and agent-relative reasons, and for the proper relation between them. But general agent-relative principles, though they must be acceptable to everyone, depend on a different kind of impersonal judgment from the one which enables us to recognize that what happens to anyone is just as important as what happens to anyone else. In addition, we have to enter into the motivational point of view of each individual and recognize that there are also conditions on what it is reasonable to demand of him, because his personal standpoint imposes certain claims. This type of judgment is still general, and it must find a form whose application to everyone at once is consistent. The results must satisfy some version of Kantian universalizability. If the aim is to discover principles of conduct which everyone can affirm that everyone should follow, they should accommodate both agent-neutral and agent-relative reasons in a livable combination.

10. For example, everyone's life has both agent-neutral and agent-relative value: Each of us has an agent-neutral reason to care about everyone, and in addition an agent-relative reason to care more particularly about himself. I have discussed this distinction in *The Possibility of Altruism*, pp. 90–95, and *The View From Nowhere*, pp. 152–54; cf. Derek Parfit, *Reasons and Persons*, p. 143.

5

Kant's Test

The condition of universalizability can take widely different forms, depending on how the practical reason of individuals is conceived. And what is reasonable for individuals cannot be determined at the level of individual practical reason alone, but depends also on some judgment about the collective result of everyone's following those principles—which individuals must take into account. The difficulty of making determinate sense of such a standard of unanimity is shared by all ideal contractualist theories, but let me illustrate it with a familiar problem from the interpretation of Kant's ethics (a version of which also arises about Scanlon's view.)

The categorical imperative states that we may act only on those maxims which we can at the same time will to be universal laws. But how are we supposed to discover, about a particular maxim, whether we can or cannot will it to be a universal law? Leaving aside the cases where we can't even *conceive* of the maxim being turned into a universal law, what does it mean to say that though we can conceive of it, we can't *will* it—that as Kant says, this would involve a contradiction in the will?

The fourth of Kant's examples in the *Foundations of the Metaphysics of Morals,* illustrating the application of the categorical imperative, presents this interpretive problem vividly. I quote it in part. The fourth man

> finds himself flourishing, but he sees others who have to struggle with great hardships (and whom he could easily help); and he thinks "What does it matter to me? Let everyone be as happy as

Heaven wills or as he can make himself; I won't deprive him of anything; I won't even envy him; only I have no wish to contribute anything to his well-being or to his support in distress!" . . . But although it is possible that a universal law of nature could subsist in harmony with this maxim, yet it is impossible to *will* that such a principle should hold everywhere as a law of nature. For a will which decided in this way would conflict with itself, since many a situation might arise in which the man needed love and sympathy from others, and in which, by such a law of nature sprung from his own will, he would rob himself of all hope of the help he wants for himself.[11]

Let me say first that a bit of philosophic license is unavoidable in reading this argument. It cannot depend on the person in comfortable circumstances thinking that he might *actually* some day find himself in dire straits, for there are people so well off and well insured that it would be completely irrational of them to take such a possibility seriously. Yet such persons are presumably supposed to be under the same duty of mutual aid as everyone else. So the thought experiment has to be understood as hypothetical, and independent of real probabilities. Even a very rich and secure person would want to be helped if he were destitute, and this remains true even if he believes the likelihood of his becoming destitute is negligible.

It seems to me clear, furthermore, that the thought experiment we are asked to perform in applying the categorical imperative positively requires us to take into account the personal standpoints of each of the parties to any situation covered by the principle under review, and their associated motives and values. We are to ask ourselves whether we can will the universalization of our maxim in light of the full range of effects and motivational demands it would entail for all the parties in whose place we imagine ourselves.

But here is the main problem. Because the situation involves a conflict of interests, *any* maxim on which a person proposes to act would, if universalized, conflict with what he would want

11. *Foundations of the Metaphysics of Morals*, p. 423.

for himself in at least *one* of the hypothetical positions he might occupy under it. The principle of no mutual aid, to be sure, contradicts what he would want if he were destitute. But a positive principle of charity contradicts his antecedent preference for keeping his money for himself. Even a destitute person, testing the universalizability of a principle of charity, would have to acknowledge that it requires some sacrifices by the better off—sacrifices which he would prefer not to have to make were he among the better off. So why doesn't *every* maxim one might propose in such a situation fail to satisfy the categorical imperative, by generating a contradiction in the will when one tries to will its universalization?

Kant claims that the maxim of strict neglect fails the test, and implies that some maxims of positive aid pass it. I believe it is significant, and part of the significance of his concept of "imperfect" or "meritorious" duty, that he apparently regards a range of levels of charity as consistent with the categorical imperative, and that the boundary between what does and does not create a contradiction in the will here is not precise. Nevertheless, we cannot understand how the categorical imperative yields any results at all in such a case unless we can interpret the idea of what it is and is not possible to will, with respect to sets of hypothetical situations in which we occupy different roles associated with all the interests that conflict. The point is that some resolutions of these conflicts of interest are supposed to be willable when we put ourselves in each person's shoes, while others are not. And everyone, taking into account all points of view, is supposed to be able to arrive at the same answers.

I shall come back to this problem, though I don't have a solution to it; but let me comment on two points here. First, the sort of question that I have said must be answered in applying the categorical imperative is itself so close to a moral question about the right way to deal with conflicting interests that it invites the suspicion that the whole procedure is empty: that the categorical imperative cannot be the basis of morality because

to derive results from it one must rely on the very moral judgments one is trying to derive.

Second, it has been proposed, by R. M. Hare,[12] that there is
a straightforward answer to the question of what can and cannot be willed as a universal law, and that utilitarianism is the
ultimate standard to which we are led by the categorical imperative. This is because he believes that the only rational way to
resolve conflicts among our imaginary interests, when we put
ourselves simultaneously in all the hypothetical positions affected by a universal law, is to add up all the advantages and
disadvantages and pick the principle which yields the most positive overall balance.

As against these two views, I shall argue that the ideal of
universal acceptability is a genuine and nonvacuous alternative
to the pure dominance of the impersonal standpoint and utilitarianism, one which allows the personal standpoint an independent role in the justification of universal principles, and which
actually explains why some solutions are morally plausible and
others not.

If we accept the duality of the self, then from the impersonal
standpoint two general judgments will emerge which there is
no obvious way of combining, viz.:

1. Everyone's life is equally important.
2. Everyone has his own life to lead.

The second judgment applies even to people who accept the
first, and it implies some limit to the extent to which anyone's
life must be controlled by the first. But likewise the first implies
some limit to the license given by the second.

How large and of what shape is the space left free for each
person under (2) from the impartial claims of value expressed
by (1)? An ethical position on this issue requires not only the
justification of choices by reference to motives, but the justification of motives as well, and of the relations among them.

12. See *Freedom and Reason*, pp. 123–24.

The relation between motivation and justification in ethical theory is a matter of controversy. My own view is that moral justification must be capable of motivating, but not in virtue of reliance on pre-moral motives. An argument can generate motives, and action, by showing someone what he has a reason to do, a reason that does not simply derive from what he already wants. Of course the arguments will depend for their effectiveness on some sort of motivational capacity of the individual, but this is to say no more than that he must be capable of understanding that these really are reasons, and of appreciating their force.

I believe the right way to try to approach a solution where existing motives lead to irreconcilable conflict is to use the demand for unanimity itself as a condition on the choice of rational principles. If we find that persons motivated by the usual mix of personal and impersonal reasons are still too far apart to be able to identify any arrangement that none of them could reasonably reject, and the principle of which can therefore be willed by everyone, that is itself a reason to reevaluate the standards of reasonableness that lead to such a result. (Here again I follow Scanlon.)

Of course such reassessment will not necessarily produce a solution. It may be that the only general principles logically capable of yielding unanimity in certain circumstances will remain plainly unacceptable to someone—either because they involve too complete a subordination of personal to impersonal values, or because they require too much deference by some to the personal motives of others. In that case there may be no alternative to a *merely* political solution—one which is forced on the recalcitrant losers by those with greater power. But if the losers have no reason to accept the result except that they are forced to, this is clearly not the best type of outcome. It would be morally preferable, and a condition of true political legitimacy, if the general principles governing agent-relative reasons limited the reach of those reasons in such a way that they left standing some solutions or distributions of advantages and disadvantages that no one could reasonably refuse, even if he were in a position to do so. Instead of morality being like politics in its sensitivity to the balance of power, we should want politics to be more like morality in its aim of unanimous acceptability.

This requires more than formal universality in the formulation of agent-relative principles—that is, the condition that each person act only on reasons that anyone else could appeal to in comparable circumstances. Even a general principle of pure selfishness would be universal in that sense. Rather, I am talking about a condition of harmony among the aims and actions of distinct persons as part of what determines which principles of agent-relative rationality are the right ones.

To apply this condition would mean that if we find that an apparently reasonable personal-impersonal balance for individuals still leads them into unresolvable conflict over the kind of basic social arrangements they can accept, we may nevertheless not regard the prosecution of this conflict as an acceptable determinant of the actual result. That is, we should not be content just to pit ourselves against our fellow humans in alliance with some but in opposition to others, and let the outcome be determined in a way the losers would be reasonable to reject if they weren't forced to accept it. Of course if they have no choice, then in a sense it is reasonable for them to accept it, but that is precisely the sort of reasonableness that the desire for ideal unanimity seeks to get beyond. We should not be satisfied with a mere bargain, if the process that leads to it does not confer on it a moral validity that makes the result immune to further moral criticism. Particularly if they are influenced by large inequalities in bargaining power at the start, some of the bargains struck or equilibria reached among apparently reasonable individuals will not seem acceptable when looked at again from outside, and this will reflect the fact that some of the parties have no reason to uphold the arrangement except that they are forced to.

The failure of reasonable unanimity thus becomes a ground for questioning the interpretation of individual reasonableness

that led to it. That is, the conditions of individual reasonableness not only have to be based on principles that can be universally acknowledged (that is true of every form of practical reason): They have in addition to be capable of harmonizing with
one another in collective and institutional forms of conduct that
can themselves be the objects of acceptance and support and
willing participation by all individuals who are reasonable by
those very standards. (This is, I believe, the essence of Kant's
concept of the kingdom of ends.)

The desire for a solution to our conflicts that at some level
everyone must accept is another expression of the recognition
that, important as one's life may be from the inside, one is only
one person among all those who exist. But in this case the recognition does not manifest itself through the detached perspective of impartiality, but through a universal identification with
the point of view of each individual, and a consequent desire
to find a way to live which can be endorsed by everyone, partly
but not entirely out of impartiality.

Pure impartiality cannot guarantee this sort of Kantian unanimity, because it does not act alone. The initial opposition between impartiality and personal aims is somewhat modified by
the internalization of impartiality as an individual motive. The
well-being of his fellow humans becomes in this way important
to each person, part of what he wants. But unless impartiality
replaces the individual's purely personal aims completely (which
is neither possible nor desirable) the mixture of impartiality and
the personal that is the usual individual configuration will continue to generate conflict among and within persons.

The demand that we settle these new conflicts ethically rather
than by political bargaining comes from the impersonal standpoint itself, which continues to generate requirements even after
one has incorporated a component of impartiality into one's
motivational scheme as a result of occupying it — only now it
assumes its Kantian form. Presented with the new situation in
which everyone is expected to recognize the claims of impartiality, one wants to know what balance it is reasonable for in-

dividuals to strike between this and their more personal aims—
and one wants to know this not just from one's own personal
point of view, but as a matter of general principle. We want to
live by principles that anyone can accept, partly but not only
on the basis of an impartial concern for everyone.

This requirement differs from the categorical imperative only
in making explicit something already implicit in it—that I can
will that everyone should adopt as a maxim only what everyone
else can also will that everyone should adopt as a maxim—for
it is clearly assumed by Kant that universalizability will yield the
same results for everyone. When we consider impersonally what
would be an acceptable form of life for beings like ourselves
who combine a common capacity for impartiality with divergent personal aims, the answer should be one that each of us
can live by and affirm as an adequate expression of both standpoints, in light of the fact that everyone else must be asked to
affirm it also.

As we know from the controversies surrounding Kant's ethical theory, it is very hard to determine what, if anything, would
be unanimously acceptable. Kant himself believed there was a
natural balance between individuality and the claims of benevolence in personal morality, and that in political theory the protection of an equal liberty for everyone would more or less meet
the requirement.[13] One can feel doubtful about these results
without feeling confident about any alternative. But whether or
not there is a general solution, it is clear that the conditions of
acceptability can be more easily met in some circumstances than
in others. So in attacking the problem political and moral theory will be linked through the attempt to devise institutions and
forms of life which, by their effects on people and their circumstances, will bring closer the possibility of a form of rationality
that leads to collective harmony.

At the moment I see no general solution to this problem.

13. See *On the Common Saying: "This May be True in Theory, but It
Does Not Apply in Practice."*

That is, there are, I suspect, no general principles governing both agent-relative, personal reasons and agent-neutral, impartial reasons, and their combination, which are acceptable from all points of view in light of their consequences under all realistically possible conditions. Under some conditions—including, I think, those of the actual world—any standards of individual conduct which try to accommodate both sorts of reasons will be either too demanding in terms of the first or not demanding enough in terms of the second.

It is part of the appeal both of pure consequentialist theories—which admit only agent-neutral reasons to morality—and of pure individual rights theories—which grant moral authority to whatever results from the interaction of individuals conducting themselves in conformity with certain agent-relative reasons—that they guarantee a right answer in every conceivable circumstance. But if we try to satisfy constraints coming from both directions, the strain may be too great, and we may be unable to find a systematic way of combining these factors which consistently yields a morally acceptable result.

Let me illustrate by returning to Kant's fourth example. A happy solution would be this: There is a modest level of aid to others in need below which a well-off person may not fall, because he cannot will such tight-fistedness as a universal law. But above that level it is at the discretion of the individual how much he will sacrifice for the benefit of others; many levels of aid are acceptable.[14]

I believe, however, that another story is closer to the truth. For suppose the well-off person sees that a great many others are in serious need, and that he could help significant numbers of them, at small cost to himself per individual, but at great cost—the cost of fundamentally changing his life and abandoning many of his personal projects—if he helps as many as he can. If we ask, about this case, what can be willed as a universal

14. A related proposal is made by Samuel Scheffler; see *The Rejection of Consequentialism,* p. 20. In that book, and in subsequent work, Scheffler explores in depth the effect on morality of the personal point of view.

law, I believe we get the following answer. It is still clearly unacceptable to fall below a modest overall level of aid to others—
taking into account both the plight of the needy and the motivational demands on the donors. But as we move above that
level we gradually enter a region where we cannot will as a
universal principle *either* that one *must or* that one *need not* help
the needy at that level of sacrifice to one's personal aims. The
attempt to apply universal agent-relative reasons rules out the
former, and impartial agent-neutral reasons rule out the latter.

If we continue on up to a very high level of individual sacrifice in aid of others, we again enter a region where there is a
definite result: Above some level we are clearly not required to
help, because we can will a moderate degree of reservation of
the personal domain as a universal principle even in light of
the full weight of the impersonal. Nevertheless, in a substantial
intermediate range, the quest for a universalizable principle that
accommodates both personal and impersonal reasons seems to
me to have no solution.

Several things seem to be going on at once here. On the part
of the well-off person, there is a simple conflict between his
personal aims and the impersonal appeal of what is best overall. This alone has no satisfactory resolution in some cases. But
then there is also the opposite conflict from the point of view
of a person in need—between his needs and his recognition of
the legitimate interest of others in living their own lives. Someone trying to identify a universalizable principle must occupy
both of these points of view, and combine them. But it seems
as if any general principle in the intermediate range could be
reasonably rejected either from the point of view of the needy,
as insufficiently generous, or from the point of view of the well-
off, as too demanding. There seems to be no principle of conduct for everyone whose collective results we can collectively
endorse.

The moral consequence is that, while everyone is obliged to
avoid the extremes whose exclusion no one could reasonably
reject, within the intermediate range between these extremes

one party or the other will be morally justified in resisting or withholding cooperation from whatever arrangement is in effect. They may have reasons of prudence or fear not to do this, but not reasons deriving from an impersonal assessment of the impact of the system on everyone, themselves included. In one way or another, some of the parties to any such arrangement will be able to object that, taking everything into account, the weight which it accords to their point of view in relation to that of everyone else is not sufficient to make it unreasonable for them to defect from the arrangement, if they can. Each individual's personal motives exercise a certain amount of centrifugal force, which can be contained up to a point by impersonal values, but only up to a point.

Of course anyone, and not just the rejecting party himself, can recognize this as a reason for denying the legitimacy of the system. But it is the rejecting party whose personal motives will lead him reasonably to oppose or defect from it—whereas others, who can see its illegitimacy but who do not have a personal complaint against it, may with equal reasonableness resist a change on the ground that any alternative which would be acceptable to the challenger is one which *they* could reasonably reject. These situations represent failures of unanimity at the highest level, and individuals are thrown back on their own points of view, not contained within a common framework which all reasonable persons must accept.

I cannot supply a general explanation of what makes it possible to will certain principles from all points of view and not possible to will others. But there do seem to me clearly to be truths of this kind, deriving from decisive independent objections which, when they conflict, do not always cancel one another out or arrange themselves in a clear order of priority. Even though they can be recognized by any single person, the fact that these claims originate in independent lives sometimes makes them recalcitrant to combination of the kind that is familiar in the case of conflict among the values of a single individual. All I can do is to hope that theory will eventually catch up with intuition here. I recognize that the claim I have made will seem strange, but it must be remembered that Kantian unanimity, for all its obscurity, is clearly a very strong condition, so that it is by no means obvious that it can be met.

But if it cannot be met in all circumstances, the natural next task for an ethical theory which takes it seriously must be to try to identify the circumstances in which it can be met, and ask how they can be achieved. We can engage in a certain amount of mutual adjustment between the claims of impartiality and individuality. But I believe that wherever we end up, so long as we are restricted to treating this as a question of personal conduct there will be circumstances in which any principle considered in light of both its collective results and its demands on each individual will be clearly unsatisfactory. It will be unsatisfactory because in one way or another it fails to heal the division of the self that results from the duality of standpoints.

Although the problems of political theory are essentially moral, their solution must be political. Political legitimacy depends on an ethical condition: that no one have reasonable grounds to object to the system. But that condition requires political theory for its interpretation. We must turn our attention to the circumstances in which people act and by which they are formed, and we must change the question from "How should we live, whatever the circumstances?" to "Under what circumstances is it possible to live as we should?"

Principles of individual conduct are not enough: The world has to cooperate. Of course one may still be faced with the question of what to do in awful circumstances in which nothing seems acceptable, but ethics and political theory need not be a seamless system that provides a single set of principles for every circumstance, decent or indecent. If the multiple demands on decent conduct for complex beings cannot be met under all conditions, then a change in the conditions, external and internal, so that those demands can be more nearly met is part of what ethics requires. Here, too, there is no guarantee of a solution. But perhaps one can get closer.

6

The Moral Division of Labor

We have now considered the problem in three different guises: how to reconcile the duality of standpoints in the individual, how to avoid utopianism in political theory, and how to define the conditions of legitimacy.

The general form of solution I think worth exploring is familiar. It consists neither in a complete invasion of the self by social values, nor in the situation of unreconstructed individuals in an institutional context that will make the pursuit of their private aims combine to generate socially desirable results, but in the design of institutions which penetrate and in part reconstruct their individual members, by producing differentiation within the self between public and private roles, and further differentiation subordinate to these.

In a sense the aim is to externalize through social institutions the most impartial requirements of the impersonal standpoint, but our support of those institutions depends on the fact that they answer to the demands of a very important part of ourselves. If the impersonal standpoint that is essential to the makeup of each of us could be given adequate expression through our respective roles in impartial collective institutions, then the problem of integration between the two standpoints in the individual might be resolved through a transformation of its terms by the effects on individual personality of those institutions. But it is essential that the effects work through internal differentiation which exploits the natural complexity of the self, rather than seeking to create a new type of human being in whom the divisions are erased.

An approach of this kind is not merely a way of balancing the claims of the two standpoints, because its object ideally is to make possible a more complete satisfaction of both of them, by altering the conditions of their expression, and allowing part of the self to expand into the surrounding world. If the most serious impersonal claims can be externalized and met through occupation of a social role, the individual can pursue his remaining personal aims within that framework with a good conscience.

But to describe these adequacy conditions on a solution is not to offer one. No such solution has been found, nor is one in sight. Of course there are no effective political institutions which take in the whole world, but the problem exists at the level of ordinary political units as well. The demands of impartiality are so great that even institutions of much narrower scope which try in any considerable degree to meet them threaten to require an inordinate takeover of the individual's life in their service—a form of general mobilization which fails to leave enough scope for the personal standpoint. Finding a way to change this situation is a central task for political theory.

Let me comment briefly by way of background on some familiar approaches to the relation between individual and collective rationality that are to be found in nonutopian political theory. My examples are Hobbes, Bentham, Hume, Rousseau, and the tradition of modern liberalism.

Hobbes did not rely on a concern for the well-being of others to motivate the individual's support for political institutions. Instead he proposed an institutional design which would be sustained entirely by each individual's concern for his own security. This concern motivates each of us both to want to live under a stable political order, and to conduct ourselves, once it has been established with adequate enforcement mechanisms, in such a way that that stability is preserved. The power of the sovereign makes it safe for each of us to obey those rules whose maintenance is a condition of the safety of all. Thus there is no motivational division between personal and impersonal standpoints in Hobbesian political theory. A single, personal motive of security is behind both our allegiance to the political order and our individual conduct within it.

Bentham forms an interesting contrast. He believed that individuals were motivated in all their actions solely by the pursuit of pleasure and the avoidance of pain for themselves. The sources of this pleasure and pain could vary greatly from person to person, and some might derive pleasure from contemplating the pleasure of others, but the most important motives, he clearly thought, were broadly egoistic. But Bentham, unlike Hobbes, was a utilitarian, so he was forced to think of the problem of institutional design as that of creating a system of incentives which would lead even hedonistic egoists to act in a way that tended collectively to maximize the general welfare, without their having to be motivated by a concern for the general welfare. The appropriate goal of social institutions would not automatically attract the support of egoistic citizens. This results in a complete divorce between the point of view of the individual acting within the institutional framework and the utilitarian point of view which determines its design.

For example Bentham was insistent on the importance, for institutional design, of what he called the "Duty and Interest junction principle." Thus he advocated that the income of governors of orphanages and poorhouses should vary inversely with the death rate among their charges.[15] But one would not expect the governors themselves to support such a policy out of the same motives which it is supposed to stimulate. Bentham assumes, shrewdly enough, that they will care less about the survival of paupers than about their own standard of living. They can only be expected to chafe under such an enlightened policy, and it would have to be instituted and maintained in place by others, either those whose interests it served or those who were made particularly unhappy by the maltreatment of

---

15. "Outline of a Work Entitled Pauper Management Improved," pp. 380–81.

orphans and paupers and who had nothing to gain from it. In this scheme the role of serving the general welfare is given to institutions rather than left to benevolent individual motivation, but there is no attempt to present the result as a way of integrating personal and impersonal motives within the individuals who occupy roles in the system. For that reason it carries the inherent danger of instability, despite its admirable hard-headedness.

In the political theories of Hume and Rousseau, on the other hand, a version of the division of standpoints plays a significant role. Hume's theory of the artificial virtues is the first clear analysis of the powerful motivational partition which makes possible the basic conventions on which social stability depends: contract, promise, property, and legal government itself. Hume recognized that it was because we were neither perfectly altruistic nor perfectly selfish that it was both necessary and possible for us to adopt those conventions. Within the stable framework which they provide, we can pursue our personal aims with security, but our adherence to the conventions themselves, while partly dependent on a sense of personal interest in the security they make possible, is supported also by a more impersonal attachment which leads us to abide by them even when a violation would not threaten our security and would serve our other interests. It is a moral motive, supplementing the personal interest that Hobbes relied on, but not so comprehensive as impartial benevolence. Hume also held that this motive emerges when we take up a detached, impersonal standpoint. In recognizing and practicing the artificial virtues together with other members of our community, we internalize the value of those very basic collective goods which can be realized only through general conformity to certain rules of conduct. It is through our participation in these conventions, rather than through individual acts, that the value most effectively expresses itself. Thus a division within the self, or a partition of motives into separate compartments, is an essential aspect of the arrangement.

In Rousseau the element of convention is less prominent, but he conspicuously conceives of membership in society as involving the formation of a special aspect of the self—one's participation in the general will—which however is not the whole of oneself and leaves the private individual free to pursue aims which are not at variance with the common good that is the object of the general will. Thus again the reconciliation of collective and individual values is accomplished within each individual soul, through the effect of citizenship on it. And again this effect does not amount to a complete takeover by the impersonal standpoint. Rousseau believed, as did Hume, that an effective and stable basis of social harmony was psychologically available.

Apart from particular philosophers, we can see the influence of the division of standpoints and the externalization of some form of impersonal value in the liberal tradition, which has proved very resilient and adaptable, despite the reverses it has suffered during this century. Liberalism takes various forms, but they all include a system of individual rights against interference of certain kinds, together with limited positive requirements of mutual aid, all institutionalized and enforced under the rule of law in a democratic regime. In the spirit of Humean moderation this is a limited morality which supports a political theory of limited government, and its support demands only a limited though significant contribution from the impersonal standpoint in each of us. Individualism and personal motives are left with considerable (negative) freedom to influence the conduct of life, and these limitations contribute to the system's psychological effectiveness.

Yet they have also made the liberal tradition unsatisfactory to many, even among those who are attached to individualistic values. By considering liberalism and its problems, we can return to the difficulty of reconciliation with which I began, because the history of liberalism is a history of gradual growth in recognition of the demands of impartiality as a condition on the legitimacy of social and political institutions. As these impersonal demands achieve broader and broader scope, they gradually come to seem overwhelming, and it becomes progressively harder to imagine a system which does justice to them as well as to the demands of individuality.

To some extent this dissatisfaction has been met by increasing the governmental functions of mutual aid, through the development of the welfare state and a social democratic version of liberal theory. But the vast inequalities of wealth and power which even the more egalitarian versions of such systems continue to generate are really incompatible with an adequate response to the impartial attitude which is the first manifestation of the impersonal standpoint. The liberal state may be better than the competition, but it is not good enough, and not just because it isn't working as intended. The wide acceptance of one or another variety of liberalism in our culture is warranted by the spectacular failure of more radical alternatives which have been inescapably revealed as utopian. But even if no other system yet devised does better, that does not mean it should be regarded as a satisfactory solution; rather it is a workable arrangement which goes some distance toward accommodating the two standpoints but is still unsatisfactory.

The question is whether a more egalitarian set of institutions can be devised which is still liberal in spirit, in that it respects the mixture of personal and impersonal aspects of each individual and uses some type of moral division of labor between social institutions and individual conduct to embody that respect, while at the same time satisfying the demands of impartiality more completely than liberalism does—even in its more egalitarian forms.

The experience of different countries supports different answers to this question. Recent developments in the United States and Britain, for example, are not encouraging, whereas the Scandinavian countries are often cited as harbingers of long-term egalitarian tendencies. Perhaps because of overexposure to the political culture of the United States, I believe that egalitarian liberalism itself contains sources of instability which tend to hinder the achievement of its humane ideals. The tension

between its public impersonal egalitarianism and its encouragement of the private pursuit of personal aims may be too sharp
to permit coherent reflection in the integrated but internally
differentiated personality of the individuals who are supposed
to embrace them both. The moral division of labor between
social institutions and the individual will work only if it corresponds to a possible division within the individual which amounts
to a coherent form of life, allowing him simultaneously to pursue his personal aims and to support the institutions which sur-
round and constrain and limit that pursuit.

But there is a definite tendency in liberal societies for the
better off—not merely a rich minority but the majority who are
not poor—to resist the pursuit of socioeconomic equality beyond a rather modest level. This is partly due to the distorting
influence on democratic politics of large concentrations of wealth,
but it also reflects a more general psychological disposition. It
may indicate limits to how egalitarian a liberal system can be.
On the other hand, it is important not to be too impressed by
the unavoidable difficulties involved in any transition to a significantly more equal system, since that may evoke resistances
of a much higher order than would arise if people were used
to it and had had their expectations formed by it. The transition problem and the stability problem are different.

Politics clearly has the potential to be more egalitarian than
individual morality. Institutions, unlike individuals, don't have
their own lives to lead. Still, they must be staffed and occupied
by real individuals who are never wholly taken up by their social roles, and for whom social roles in any case have personal
as well as social significance. This is not just a practical limitation. The individuals among whom one aspect of morality requires us to be impartial are essentially and valuably distinct
and different, and the value of each of their lives depends on
its value to them, as it is led from the inside. As we approach
the personal core, each person's reason to lead his own life ex-
ercises a stronger and stronger agent-relative claim, even if other
people's ability to pursue *their* own lives would be furthered if

the claim were disallowed. The protection of individuality for its own sake is as important a condition on political theory as is equality—a condition that must be met for each individual—and it, too, is a moral requirement. It seems to me that none of the currently available forms of collective life does anything like justice to them both, and that it is imperative to bring such a possibility into existence.

A better solution will have to provide more impersonally acceptable ways for us to express our individuality, and this would necessarily involve changes in the conceptions we have of ourselves, and in our motives. It cannot be accomplished by the growth of altruism alone, though I don't want to deny the value of this, or its possibility. Apart from the purely motivational obstacles, altruism is too general a motive to run a society with. Most productive activities require concentration on much more special tasks and projects and the carrying out of specialized functions. So the attention and motivation of individuals has to be focused on their immediate surroundings and success in their particular endeavors. This cannot in general be accomplished unless they are connected with personal aims. Wider concerns are better met by a sense that the overall system in which individuals play a part is a decent one, so that in leading their lives they are neither benefiting from nor ignoring the avoidable misery of others—nor are others doing this with respect to them.

But this requires a greater penetration of the character of individual life by institutional and conventional structures which serve the good of everyone in a morally acceptable manner. Although people can change, they do not change most effectively and en masse through personal conversion, but through the development of practices which form their sense of themselves and make it natural for them to be guided by different priorities and values, different requirements and inhibitions. Rousseau's image of the social contract returning to each of us a reconstructed self can be adapted to more articulated forms of socialization.

The idea of a moral division of labor between individuals

and institutions is not a solution, but only the form of a solution. A workable system must define a set of overlapping roles which can engage in a realistic way with structures of individual motivation. They will include general roles such as citizen, voter, and taxpayer, as well as particular roles in the economy, the professions, the military, the educational system, the governmental bureaucracy, and the judicial system. Any given individual's identity will involve more than one of these, as well as his personal position in a family, a religion, or a cultural, racial, or ethnic subcommunity. The competition for each individual's motivational allegiance is inevitably severe. But if in addition we require that the political and economic structure in which these roles are embedded should meet a high standard of impartiality in its effects on the equally valuable lives of all participants, the potential conflicts are even greater. We begin to approach the case of the last life-jacket as opposed to the case of the last eclair.

To design institutions which serve an ideal of egalitarian impartiality without demanding a too extensive impartiality of the individuals who occupy instrumental roles in those institutions is the great unsolved problem of egalitarian political theory, social democracy, and the anti-authoritarian left in general. It is far easier to demand a more limited impartiality from the system, since this can be achieved through institutions which demand of their participants a more specialized and therefore more tenacious attachment to certain limited rights and procedures.

Liberal societies have succeeded to the extent that liberal institutions and conventions have proved psychologically comfortable and habit-forming. Where internal divisions and inequalities are not too severe and fanaticism not too great, we find that representative democracy, the rule of law, an independent judiciary, protection of personal liberties, honest bureaucratic administration relatively free of nepotism, and limited public provision financed by taxes that are not universally evaded are capable of drawing the support and cooperation of large and heterogeneous populations. The value of all this is very great, and only a fool would be in favor of sacrificing any of it. To put it into practice in most of the world would be a phenomenal achievement. But we are perhaps not at the end of human history, and it would be desirable if equally functional institutions, which individuals could come to find natural, could take us further toward an accommodation of the two standpoints. In what follows I shall discuss some specific political issues from this perspective.

7

Egalitarianism

Modern political theories agree that a society must treat its members equally in some respects, but they disagree over the respects, and the priorities among them. For someone accustomed to the forms of equality before the law and equality of citizenship that hold first place in a liberal democracy, the natural question is how far it is desirable or possible to extend the rule of equality into the areas of social and economic relations.

This topic has been extensively discussed, and most of what I have to say is not new. I shall present a case for wishing to extend the reach of equality in a legitimate political system beyond what is customary in modern welfare states, and then reflect on the great difficulties, practical and moral, of doing so. I am drawn to a strongly egalitarian social ideal, to whose realization the duality of standpoints seems to present great obstacles. So I do not see how to embody it in a morally and psychologically viable system.

Rawls devotes considerable discussion to the motivational viability of an egalitarian position in the final chapters of *A Theory of Justice*, but I find myself unable to share his psychological expectations. Essentially, my doubts lead me to suspect that Kantian unanimity may not be available over this issue. We can get closer through political institutions, but a gap remains which can be closed only by a human transformation that seems, at the moment, utopian, or by institutional invention beyond anything that is at present imaginable.

It is the motive of impartiality which gives us a reason for

wanting more equality than we have. If impartiality is not ad-
mitted as an important motive in determining the acceptability
of a social system—if every such system is just a bargain struck
among self-interested parties—then there will be no call for
equality except to the extent needed to ensure stability. But I
believe that impartiality emerges from an essential aspect of the
human point of view, and that it naturally seeks expression
through the institutions under which we live.

There are other ways to conceive of ethics and political theory. If one defines their subject matter solely in terms of the
search for possible points of agreement among distinct persons
on how they should conduct themselves, important results may
be found in the convergence of interests and the striking of
bargains for mutual advantage. But it does not disparage the
importance of these factors to insist that they are not all we
have to rely on, and that a direct concern for others is potentially the most transformative influence on the acceptability of
social ideals.

We are so accustomed to great social and economic inequalities that it is easy to become dulled to them. But if everyone
matters just as much as everyone else, it is appalling that the
most effective social systems we have been able to devise permit
so many people to be born into conditions of harsh deprivation
which crush their prospects for leading a decent life, while many
others are well provided for from birth, come to control substantial resources, and are free to enjoy advantages vastly beyond the conditions of mere decency. The mutual perception
of these material inequalities is part of a broader inequality of
social status, personal freedom, and self-respect. Those with high
income, extensive education, inherited wealth, family connections, and genteel employment are served and in many cultures
treated deferentially by those who have none of these things.
One cannot ignore the difficulties of escaping from this situation, but that is no reason not to dislike it.

The impartial attitude is, I believe, strongly egalitarian both
in itself and in its implications. As I have said, it comes from
our capacity to take up a point of view which abstracts from

who we are, but which appreciates fully and takes to heart the value of every person's life and welfare. We put ourselves in each person's shoes and take as our preliminary guide to the value we assign to what happens to him the value which it has from his point of view. This gives to each person's well-being very great importance, and from the impersonal standpoint everyone's primary importance, leaving aside his effect on the welfare of others, is the same.

The result is an enormous set of values deriving from individual lives, without as yet any method of combining them or weighing them against one another when they conflict, as they inevitably will in the real world. The question whether impartiality is egalitarian in itself is the question whether the correct method of combination will include a built-in bias in favor of equality, over and above the equality of importance that everyone's life has in the initial set of values to be combined.

Even if impartiality were not in this sense egalitarian in itself, it would be egalitarian in its distributive consequences because of the familiar fact of diminishing marginal utility. Within any person's life, an additional thousand dollars added to fifty thousand will be spent on something less important than an additional thousand added to five hundred—since we satisfy more important needs before less important ones. And people are similar enough in their basic needs and desires so that something roughly comparable holds between one person and another: Transferable resources will usually benefit a person with less more than they will benefit a person with significantly more. So if everyone's benefit counts the same from the impersonal standpoint, and if there is a presumption in favor of greater benefit, there will be a reason to prefer a more equal to a less equal distribution of a given quantity of resources. Although actual alternatives do not in general offer a constant quantity of resources, the rate at which marginal utility diminishes is so rapid that it will still have egalitarian consequences even in many cases in which the better off stand to lose more resources than the worse off stand to gain.

But I believe that impartiality is also egalitarian in itself, and that is a more controversial claim. What it means is that impartiality generates a greater interest in benefiting the worse off than in benefiting the better off—a kind of priority to the former over the latter. Of course impartiality means a concern for everyone's good, so added benefit is desirable, whoever gets it. But when it comes to a choice of whom to benefit, there is still the question of how to combine distinct and conflicting claims, and the pure idea of concern for everyone's good does not answer it.

The answer will depend on many things. We may be able to benefit more persons or fewer, and we may be able to benefit them to a greater or lesser extent. Both of these efficiency factors are certainly relevant, and impartiality will favor the first alternative over the second in each case, other things being equal. But in addition, I believe that the proper form of equal concern for all will sometimes favor benefit to the worse off even when numbers or quantity go the other way. Such a ranking of concern is internal to the attitude, correctly understood, giving the worst off a priority in their claim on our concern.[16]

The reason is that concern for everyone has to be particularized: It must contain a separate and equal concern for each person's good. When we occupy the impersonal standpoint, our impartial concern for each person exists side by side with our concern for every other person. These concerns should not be conglomerated. Even though we cannot contain all these separate lives together in our imagination, their separateness must be preserved somehow in the system of impersonal values which impartiality generates.

The point is famously made by Rawls in his charge that utilitarianism does not take seriously the distinction between per-

16. Derek Parfit, in *On Giving Priority to the Worse Off*, calls this form of egalitarianism the Pure Priority View, to distinguish it from an attachment to equality which is a pure aversion to inequality—even inequality which benefits the worst off—and which he calls Relational Egalitarianism. Later I shall discuss a further factor—a form of fairness—which lends support to this second, stronger type of egalitarianism under some conditions.

sons.[17] Rawls's construal of the moral attitude that underlies the sense of justice, as modeled in the Original Position, includes this strongly individualized impartial concern as an essential element. Because we are asked to choose principles without knowing who we are, we must put ourselves fully into the position of each representative person in the society. While the results of this simultaneous multiple identification may be obscure, it is clearly one of the sources of the egalitarian character of his theory.

This is connected with its Kantian inspiration, even though Kant himself did not draw egalitarian conclusions from the condition of treating each individual as an end in himself. If we try to view things simultaneously from everyone's point of view, as Kant insisted, we are led, I think, in an egalitarian direction. I believe this egalitarian feature is present even in pure, detached benevolence, but it also takes us part of the way toward the conditions of universal acceptability demanded by Kantian universalization: Up to a point, more equality makes it harder for anyone to object.

The fundamental point about individualized impartial concern is that it generates a large set of separate values corresponding to separate lives, and we must then make a further judgment about how to decide the inevitable conflicts among them. We cannot simply assume that they are to be combined like vectors of force, which add together or cancel one another out. That is the utilitarian solution, but it seems in fact the wrong way to treat them. Instead they have to be compared with one another at least partly in accordance with some standard of relative priority.

The separateness of the concerns does not rule out all ranking of alternatives involving different persons, nor does it mean that benefiting more people is not in itself preferable to benefiting fewer. But it does introduce a significant element of nonaggregative, pairwise comparison between the persons affected

17. *A Theory of Justice*, p. 27.

by any choice or policy, whereby the situation of each and the potential gains of each are compared separately with those of every other. I believe that when this is done, on careful reflection, a ranking of urgency naturally emerges. The claims on our impartial concern of an individual who is badly off present themselves as having some priority over the claims of *each* individual who is better off: as being ahead in the queue, so to speak. And this means there is reason to try to satisfy them first, even at some loss in efficiency, and therefore even beyond the already significant preference that derives from the diminishing marginal utility of resources. (In any case, some of those who are badly off may be suffering from other evils than poverty, and may be *inefficient* targets of resource allocation.)

To some extent the combined claims of larger numbers, or of greater quantity of benefit—particularly if it is greater not just absolutely but relative to what is already there—can pull in the contrary direction. I do not suggest that impartiality imposes an absolute priority for benefit to the worse off. But it includes some priority of this kind as a significant element, and it should incline us to favor the alternative that is least unacceptable to the persons to whom it is most unacceptable.[18]

This is a direct consequence of what I take to be the proper form of imaginative identification with the points of view of others, when we recognize their importance from the impersonal standpoint. Instead of combining all their experiences into an undifferentiated whole, or choosing as if we had an equal chance of being any of them, we must try to think about it as if we were each of them separately—as if each of their lives were our only life. Even though this is a tall order and does not describe a logical possibility, I believe it means something imaginatively and morally: It belongs to the same moral outlook that requires unanimity as a condition of legitimacy.

Pure impartiality is intrinsically egalitarian, then, in the sense

18. There is some discussion of this idea in the chapter called "Equality" in *Mortal Questions*, pp. 122–25. In that essay I also explore the connection between egalitarianism and the requirement of unanimity.

of favoring the worse off over the better off. It is not egalitarian in the sense of begrudging advantages to the better off which cost the worse off nothing, since impartial concern is universal. But for more than one reason the impersonal standpoint generates an attitude of impartiality which attracts us strongly to a social ideal in which large inequalities in the distribution of resources are avoided if possible, and in which development of this possibility is an important aim. And economic inequality is only part of the story. It may support stifling social stratification and class or communal oppression, inequality of political rights, and so forth. These are evils to which the equal concern of impartiality responds, favoring those at the bottom of the heap and those institutions which improve their status. All this comes from putting oneself in everyone's shoes, and even if we leave unspecified the strength of the egalitarian factor, measured by these standards the world is clearly a pretty terrible place.

One might of course agree that the world is a pretty terrible place without subscribing to an egalitarianism as general as I have proposed. One might say that all the moral intuitions of which we can be confident would be fully accounted for by a principle of priority to those who are not only worse off than others, but absolutely deprived, because their basic needs for food, shelter, health, and minimal self-respect are not met. This is certainly a possible view, and it could be thought that a more general egalitarianism gains unwarranted support from its overlap with such a requirement of priority to the satisfaction of absolute needs. However, I want to defend the stronger priority of worse over better off, for two reasons.

First, it seems to me intuitively right. Remember that the subject of an egalitarian principle is not the distribution of particular rewards to individuals at some time, but the prospective quality of their lives as a whole, from birth to death (a point stressed by Rawls). Contemplating the differences in life prospects at birth which are built into any system of social stratification, I do not think that our sense of priority for improvements in the position of those lower down on the scale is exhausted by the case of the absolutely needy. Of course they have first priority. But the distinction between the unskilled and the skilled working class, or between the lower middle class and the upper middle class, or between the middle class and the upper class, presents the same intuitive ranking of relative importance.

The only point at which I think it gives out is in the upper reaches of the economic distribution: My moral instincts reveal no egalitarian priority for the well-to-do over the rich and super-rich. But I suspect that is because the marginal utility of wealth diminishes so steeply in those regions (am I being hopelessly unimaginative?) that these categories do not correspond to significant objective differences in well-being, of a kind that is morally important or a serious object of impartial concern. Apart from the separate question of political power, the difference in life prospects between the children of a multimillionaire and the children of a middle-rank manager or professional are morally insignificant. On the other hand differences between the lives of skilled laborers and middle-class managers are substantial, even if neither of them is in serious need.

My second reason for favoring a general egalitarianism is that it is supported by the best theoretical interpretation of impartiality, in terms of individualized concern. The resulting method of pairwise comparison with priority going to the lower member of the pair simply does not cease to apply above the level of basic needs. I conclude that only the rejection of impartiality or another interpretation of it would warrant the rejection of a broad egalitarianism in favor of the more limited principle of abolishing absolute deprivation.[19]

19. One such interpretation might be the pure contractualism favored by Scanlon—though it is stretching a point to describe this as a principle of impartiality. I myself believe that the unanimity requirement of Scanlon's contractualism has to be supplemented by a motive of impartial egalitarian concern—assumed as a component of reasonable human motivation—in order to determine what it is and is not reasonable for individuals to reject. Scanlon has suggested that the desire to achieve unanimity might by itself supply a substan-

To embody egalitarian values in a political ideal would be an involved task. An essential part of that task would be to introduce an appropriate condition of non-responsibility into the specification of those goods and evils whose equal possession is desirable. What seems bad is not that people should be unequal in advantages or disadvantages generally, but that they should be unequal in the advantages or disadvantages for which they are not responsible. Only then must priority be given to the interests of the worse off. Two people born into a situation which gave them equal life chances can end up leading lives of very different quality as a result of their own free choices, and that should not be objectionable to an egalitarian. But to make sense of such a condition generates notorious problems.

First, there is wide disagreement over when an individual is responsible for what happens to him, ranging from disputes over freedom of the will in general to disputes over the conditions of knowledge and opportunity needed to confer responsibility for an outcome, to disputes over when the use of a natural ability or fortunate circumstance for which one is not responsible nevertheless makes one responsible for the results. These are large issues of moral philosophy into which I shall not enter here. They may themselves bring up considerations of equality in their treatment. Let me simply say that it seems to me clear that, whatever remotely plausible positive condition of responsibility one takes as correct, many of the important things in life—especially the advantages and disadvantages with which people are born or which form the basic framework within which they must lead their lives—cannot be regarded as goods or evils for which they are responsible, and so fall under the egalitarian principle.

Second, there is a problem of consistency. If A gains a benefit for which he is responsible, becoming better off than B, who is not responsible for the change, the resulting inequality

---

tial motive for eliminating serious inequalities—which the worse off can reject and the better off cannot reasonably insist on. But I believe this yields a more limited egalitarianism than I would favor.

is still acceptable, since the principle does not object to *inequalities* for which the parties are not responsible, but only to the parties' being unequal in goods or evils for *the possession of which* they are not responsible—where merely having less than someone else is not in itself counted as an evil. So if A and B are each responsible for how much of a particular good he has, the non-responsibility condition fails and inequality is unobjectionable. It is perfectly all right if A has more of the good, even though B is not responsible for the inequality, since he is not responsible for how much A has.

But suppose A gains a benefit for which he *is* responsible, but that in addition to benefiting A, A's gain positively harms B in a way for which B is *not* responsible (by taking away all his customers or simply making him poor). If the evil for which B is not responsible is always allowed to dominate the good for which A is responsible, rendering the inequality unacceptable, very little will be left. Yet there are cases in which such dominance seems undeniable: Sometimes, for example, inequalities in the conditions of children are clearly not rendered acceptable by the fact that they result from advantages and disadvantages for which their parents are responsible.

This is by way of preliminary acknowledgment that any egalitarian social theory will have to be complex, even though its impersonal sources will certainly demand significant equality as a component of the social ideal. I shall return to these complexities later, since they present major obstacles to the pursuit of equality. But at this point I want to move on to the other side of the story.

In addition to the impersonal standpoint, each of us in reality occupies his own shoes, and we must ask therefore of any concrete social ideal designed to serve the value of equality what it will be like for each of the individuals involved to live under it. The impersonal standpoint and the impartial attitudes that emerge from it form only part of their makeup. Therefore no social system can be run on the motive of impartiality alone. Nor can it be run on the assumption that individuals are motivated by a mixture of personal and impersonal attitudes in which impartiality invariably has the dominant role. A human society is not a community of saints. Whatever else they do, people will lead their own lives, and an egalitarian ideal can be approached only by creating a system which is more impartial and more egalitarian than they are, taken as whole persons. Such a system will engage their impartiality but it must operate in a way that is consistent with the other things that are true of them.

This topic can be divided into two parts. First, there is the question of the basis for allegiance of complex individuals to an impartial system as a whole. Second, there is the question of how, as individuals, they will be motivated in playing the roles which it assigns to them. This second question in turn has two aspects, the political and the personal.

I shall leave the exact strength of the egalitarian preference vague. The absolute priority to the worst off of Rawls's Difference Principle is one version, and it can be generalized into the Lexical Difference Principle, suggested by Rawls and modified by Scanlon.[20] I am inclined toward a somewhat weaker preference for the worse off, which can be outweighed by sufficiently large benefit to sufficiently large numbers of those better off.[21]

---

20. See John Rawls, *A Theory of Justice*, p. 83, and T. M. Scanlon, "Rawls' Theory of Justice." Scanlon's formulation, which he attributes to Bruce Ackerman, is as follows:

> First maximize the income, wealth, etc. of the worst-off representative person, then seek to minimize the number of people in his position (by moving them upwards); then proceed to do the same for the next worst-off social position, then the next and so on, finally seeking to maximize the benefits of those in the best-off position (as long as this does not affect the others). (p. 197 in Daniels)

21. Some may even be attracted by a more strongly egalitarian principle which warrants the reduction of inequalities even if it would worsen somewhat the absolute situation of the worst off—perhaps in the service of an ideal of solidarity. See Lawrence Crocker, "Equality, Solidarity, and Rawls' Maximin." I shall say something about this possibility later; it seems to me not to be part of the ideal of impartiality, but to involve a separate objection to a particular kind of unfairness.

On the other hand I am concerned with the problem of altering those features of individual motivation and human interaction which make it necessary to accept large inequalities in
order to benefit the worse off. The kind of egalitarianism I am
talking about would require a system much more equal than
now exists in most democratic countries.

8

Problems of Convergence

Let me begin by asking whether the duality of standpoints threatens the rejection in advance of any social ideal embodying a strong condition of equality—leaving aside for the moment the problems of its realization. Let us suppose for the sake of this part of the argument that some system of radically progressive taxation and public provision under capitalism, or some not-yet-invented form of market socialism, would be optimal in realizing such an ideal. The question then is whether people as they are actually constituted could be expected to support it. I intend this not as an empirical but as a moral question, to be addressed in the Kantian mode. What sort of accommodation, if any, between egalitarian impartiality and personal motivation can pass the test of acceptability (in the sense of nonrejectability) from all points of view at once?

To consider this question we must descend from the level of egalitarian impartiality and regard things instead from the mixed point of view of real members of a society. Any strongly egalitarian system will be one of a number of alternative possible arrangements, known to the participants, under each of which some of them would do better and others worse. The problem of unanimous acceptability concerns the comparison among these alternatives. If someone can reasonably reject one of them, it must mean that it is reasonable for him to refuse to give up one of the others. Now a strongly egalitarian system will clearly not be rejected by the worst off, who would do even worse in a less equal system. And the worse off may have reasonable grounds for rejecting any system that is significantly less equal. But at this point I won't concentrate on that side of the ledger, but will instead consider the position of the better off. They are the ones whose potential objections to an egalitarian system must be answered if it is to be established as legitimate—as unreasonable for anyone to reject.

The question is, why shouldn't their impartiality be tempered with a substantial dose of self-interest, or other personal motives, in determining what alternatives they are and are not willing to forgo? The only people who won't experience this conflict with regard to strong equality are the worst off, whose claims get priority and whose personal interests—provided they are not in competition with one another—coincide with the demands of egalitarian impartiality. Why should others accept this? Can't they complain that such a system is not truly impartial, since it asks something of them that it does not ask of everyone—namely the sacrifice of their personal aims and interests for the benefit of others? I have put the objection in this general, ethical form because I wish to leave aside the purely personal complaint against an arrangement, that it doesn't do enough for *me*. That is not a complaint that can be offered to others, unless it conceals a more general argument which one would be willing to recognize if someone else offered it.

In evaluating this objection to strong egalitarianism as asking too much, we should have in mind some alternatives. Naturally we can't consider them all, and I shall leave aside objections which give no weight to claims of interpersonal concern. I shall also assume that all the serious candidates include a strictly protected sphere of basic personal rights and liberties—freedom of conscience, freedom of association, freedom of expression, rights of due process, and so forth—without which (as will be argued in a later chapter) no system would be universally acceptable. This will be true of the strongly egalitarian system as well as of its rivals.[22] The question then is whether some alter-

22. This is Rawls's procedure when making what he calls the "second fun-

native to the strongly egalitarian distributive component of such a system is superior in meeting the condition of universal acceptability for persons of the usual divided sort.

To simplify, let us suppose that an objector might have either of two alternative types of system in mind which he believes would be more justifiable. One is the system obtained by keeping the personal rights constant and replacing strong egalitarianism with a utilitarian standard, which is impartial among individuals but combines their claims in cases of conflict by always favoring the maximization of benefit, calculated by quantity of benefit and numbers affected. This can be called *restricted utilitarianism*.[23] The other system the objector might have in mind is one which is impartial but more limited in range—not with respect to people's well-being in general but with respect to goods regarded as basic. These would include not only personal rights and liberties, but certain conditions of security, self-respect, and fulfillment of basic material needs which are to be guaranteed to everyone equally. I will call this the *guaranteed minimum*. It too would answer to a kind of equal concern, but of a more limited nature.

In both cases the objector would claim that it is reasonable for him to reject the strong egalitarian solution because, by contrast with the alternative, it imposes an unfair burden of acceptance on individuals like him who stand to sacrifice something under it. If the contrast is with restricted utilitarianism, the claim is that it is unreasonable to impose an asymmetrical standard of sacrifice on the better off and the worse off, requiring the former to sacrifice more in order to avoid the latter having to sacrifice less. If the contrast is with the guaranteed minimum, the claim is that it is unreasonable to ask those with superior wealth or earning power to accept sacrifices for others

---

damental comparison" between the difference principle and the principle of average utility from the point of view of the original position. See *Justice as Fairness*, p. 96, and the earlier "Reply to Alexander and Musgrave," pp. 646–50.

23. Rawls uses the term *restricted utility* for a similar idea.

unless it will provide them with what is really essential—though for the sake of such benefits, substantial sacrifices are reasonable.

Let me take up the utilitarian challenge first. Part of the appeal of that alternative depends on an attraction in principle to value-maximization as the correct way of combining concerns for many different persons when they come into conflict. As I have said, this method does not attract me because I believe pairwise comparison is an ineliminable aspect of the right attitude to many distinct people about all of whom we are equally concerned. It should be an internal feature of any form of benevolence. The reason for this has to do with the proper interpretation of strict impartiality, and I shall not add to what I have said about it. We are now concerned with the issue from the standpoint of the motivational burdens on individuals of accepting the two alternative systems. By comparison with restricted utilitarianism, I believe, an egalitarian principle is at an advantage with respect to the equity of the motivational burdens it imposes.

The utilitarian idea is that we all count equally at the primary level, and any of us may have to accept sacrifices if the benefits they yield to others are large enough to outweigh them. For reasons of efficiency this will more often involve sacrifices by the well off in favor of the badly off; but the only reason for this is efficiency in maximizing the total benefit, and if that reason is absent, there is no other reason to refrain from benefiting the better off at the expense of the worse off. Each party will be sorry when it is his turn to accept a sacrifice, but everyone is being treated the same and no one has special ground for complaint.

This is plausible in the abstract but not, I think, correct, because it ignores the following fundamental psychological fact: It is easier to accept sacrifices or forgo advantages for the sake of those worse off than you than for the sake of those better off than you.

This simple idea, I believe, lies behind one of Rawls's arguments for the egalitarian difference principle, though it is obscure in Rawls's exposition, so that the argument looks initially defective. The difference principle, recall, permits the first, top-down kind of sacrifice through the institutions of distributive justice but not the second, bottom-up kind. Utilitarianism permits both. The issue is whether the two sorts of sacrifice are symmetrical. Rawls criticizes utilitarianism for imposing an unreasonable burden of acceptance on some individuals, precisely the objection which we have been imagining a utilitarian to make against the egalitarian position. Here is what Rawls says:

> The principles of justice apply to the basic structure of the social system and to the determination of life prospects. What the principle of utility asks is precisely a sacrifice of these prospects. We are to accept the greater advantages of others as a sufficient reason for lower expectations over the whole course of our life. This is surely an extreme demand. In fact, when society is conceived as a system of cooperation designed to advance the good of its members, it seems quite incredible that some citizens should be expected, on the basis of political principles, to accept lower prospects of life for the sake of others.[24]

This seems to invite the reply that the difference principle is vulnerable to exactly the same objection, since it requires the more talented or fortunate to accept lower expectations over the whole course of their lives for the sake of others.[25] But what Rawls clearly means is that it is an extreme demand to have to accept the *greater* advantages of others—in the sense of *advantages greater than one enjoys oneself*—as a sufficient reason for lower expectations over the whole course of one's life. His position implies that he does *not* think it an extreme demand to have to accept lower expectations for the sake of others who will be better off than they would otherwise have been, but still not as well off as you are. That is accepting lower life prospects

24. *A Theory of Justice,* p. 178.
25. An objection of this kind is made by Robert Nozick in *Anarchy, State, and Utopia,* pp. 195–97, and I made it myself in "Rawls on Justice" (p. 13 in Daniels).

for the *advantage* of others, but not for the *greater* advantages of others.

This has both motivational and moral plausibility. In a way, it is the emotional equivalent at the participant level of pairwise comparison as a method of combining distinct claims viewed impersonally. I don't believe the point can carry enough weight to yield the difference principle for all imaginable cases, since the demand in the other direction can't be written off entirely, and in very disproportionate cases it might not be unreasonable for the better off to rebel. But the point is certainly of value in defending the asymmetry of top-down and bottom-up sacrifice against the utilitarian alternative. Egalitarian impartiality is both theoretically more plausible and motivationally more reasonable than utilitarian impartiality.

Nevertheless, when the two imply different results, as in the case where a minority underclass could be helped only at the cost of a quantitatively larger aggregate sacrifice by a large middle class, the lesser motivational burden imposed by egalitarianism will be felt by more people than the greater motivational burden imposed by restricted utilitarianism. That is one of many reasons why equality has such a hard time in modern democracies.

Let us move to the objection from the standpoint of the guaranteed minimum, which would regard the claims of both egalitarianism and utilitarianism as extravagant. The idea is that what each person owes to all others is nonaggression, honest dealing, and a concern limited to the basic conditions of a decent existence rather than for their well-being in general. While it is reasonable for anyone to reject a system which does not guarantee him this much, it is not reasonable to reject a system because it fails to provide one with advantages beyond this, and it *is* reasonable to reject a system which requires one to forgo benefits merely in order to provide others with advantages above the required minimum. Hence the better off can reject equality in favor of the guaranteed minimum, and the worse off cannot reject the guaranteed minimum in favor of more equality.

The first thing to be said about this argument is that it contains a fatal mistake.[26] It is simply false that the worse off cannot reasonably reject the guaranteed minimum by reference to the standard proposed. If they were to accept it, forgoing a more egalitarian system, they would be forgoing benefits above the minimum for themselves, merely in order to avoid depriving the better off of the benefits *they* can enjoy only under the guaranteed minimum, and which they would not enjoy under a more equal system. Those benefits to the better off are of course well above the required minimum. So if the better off can refuse to accept a sacrifice merely in order to provide the worse off with such benefits, the worse off are in exactly the same position: They too can refuse to accept the sacrifice of benefits above the guaranteed minimum merely in order to provide the better off with such benefits. The objection illegitimately privileges the guaranteed minimum (or perhaps laissez-faire) as the "normal" condition relative to which sacrifice is to be identified, whereas in fact each of the two systems being compared provides one of the parties with benefits above the minimum at the expense of the other.

This means that the proposed standard of reasonable rejection would result immediately in the failure of both systems, the guaranteed minimum and egalitarianism, to meet the test of unanimous nonrejectability. Neither of them could be defended as a legitimate arrangement, and in fact every possible arrangement would fail the test, so long as there were any differences between them in how they benefited different parties above the minimum.

Now I have already indicated that I believe there may be cases in which no legitimate solution to the problem of conflicting interests is available, so that parties are reduced to trying to impose their personally preferred solution by whatever power they may be able to muster—against the reasonable opposition of their opponents. But I do not believe that the breakdown

---

26. Which was pointed out to me by G. A. Cohen.

described here is an example of this, because I do not believe that the standard of rejectability on which it depends is a reasonable one.

Specifically, it is not reasonable for the better off to reject systems significantly more equal than the guaranteed minimum, on the ground that the sacrifice demanded of them by such systems is excessive. Such a standard does not ask enough of our impartiality, as applied to the choice of a social ideal. The concern for others that arises from the impersonal standpoint is far more comprehensive than a respect for those basic needs recognized in traditional liberal democracies of the less generous type, even if it does not take in absolutely everything that people want.

If I am right, then a system limited to meeting those needs can be rejected by the worse off and cannot be insisted upon by the better off. The former are being asked to accept a low standard of living on the ground that it would be an intolerable burden on the winners further to reduce their after-tax income merely to give the losers more. This seems hardly reasonable. The latter, if they sense this, will be partly compensated for their social unease by the very advantages which make them on reflection uneasy, and can drown their fellow feeling in claret. But if they really put themselves in the shoes of the losers, they must recognize the legitimacy of resentment, unless they rationalize uncontrollably. They cannot plausibly claim that the losers should recognize, when they put themselves in the shoes of the winners, that it is unreasonable to ask them to sacrifice the rewards of their efforts and position which such a system affords, merely for the sake of others who are worse off and whose lives could be significantly improved under an alternative system.

On the other hand, while the guaranteed minimum is not satisfactory, it raises an issue which cannot be ignored, and which is underrated by both the utilitarian and the egalitarian positions, even in the qualified form I have specified in which basic personal rights and liberties are strictly protected. Individuals want something for themselves from their society, as well as wanting something for everyone, themselves included. If its design appeals too exclusively to their impartiality, whether this is egalitarian or utilitarian, it will leave a large section of their motives out of account.

This is not merely a practical problem. Each person can recognize that the same thing is true of everyone, so there is an ethical question of how the satisfaction or refusal of these conflicting personal claims on society can be equitably determined. If we wish to let our personal point of view affect our attitudes in a way that is not objectionable, it must be in accordance with conditions which we judge would be reasonable for anyone. And it is clear that in a world not inhabited by perfect altruists, some account must be taken, not just for practical but for moral reasons, of how different social arrangements look from the perspectives of the differently situated participants.

This factor creates some pressure to modify the claims of egalitarian impartiality in determining the basic structure of society, though the results are far from clear. Before taking this up, however, let me say two further things about what is wrong with the answer given by the guaranteed minimum. I believe that position owes whatever appeal it has to the displacement of moral standards that are appropriate within an acceptable social framework, to the quite different task of evaluating the framework itself.

First, it clearly is a desirable feature of a social order that within it, people should not be too constrained in the pursuit of their own lives by constant demands for impartial attention to the welfare of others. A limited morality of noninterference; respect for life, liberty, and property; and mutual aid only of the most basic sort embodies this idea effectively. But this is an adequate individual morality *only within the context of a societal framework that does much more* to satisfy the claims of impartial concern which other lives make on us. It is completely illegitimate to take this morality out of such a context and use it as the sole standard to determine what we owe one another through the operation of the social framework *within* which we may with good conscience live our personal lives by those minimal rules.

The second point is this. When we follow those rules within an acceptable social system, it is part of the freedom they confer on us that we do not have to feel responsible for everything that happens which we could have prevented. The lack of a washing machine by the family next door is not even in part my doing or my responsibility just because I could have bought them one. But I believe that such restrictions on what is usually called negative responsibility do not apply in the same way to our relations to one another through our common social institutions, especially an involuntary institution such as the state, together with its economic structure. We are responsible, through the institutions which require our support, for the things they could have prevented as well as for the things they actively cause. That is why the worse off, under the guaranteed minimum, are being asked to sacrifice for the benefit of the better off, just as surely as the better off are asked to sacrifice for the benefit of the worse off under an egalitarian system. If sacrifice is measured by comparison with possible alternatives rather than by comparison with the status quo, the situations of possible winners and possible losers are symmetrical. So an acceptable societal framework for apportioning negative interpersonal responsibilities is a condition of the moral acceptability of strict limitations on negative responsibility in the rules of individual conduct that govern personal relations within it.

These claims about responsibility are moral, not causal. I shall say more about them later. But now I want to take up again the issue of how the personal-impersonal balance may be struck, and to do so in a way suggested by the discussion so far—returning to the idea of the moral division of labor as the place where one might most plausibly look for an answer. This will be followed by discussion of the obstacles to an egalitarian outcome.

9

Problems of Structure

A natural suggestion would be that the constraints deriving from the personal standpoint enter more appropriately into the determination of what may be asked of people as participants in the system, when they are making choices about how to lead their lives and what to do on particular occasions, than into the determination of the distribution of benefits by the operation of the system as a whole. For general acceptance of the basic structure and its results, impartiality should be far more important, even though the accommodation of different standpoints through some sort of convergence will also play a role.

In that case, ideally, the main influence of the personal standpoint in determining acceptability would concern the character of individual life within the framework of the basic structure—how personal aims, interests, and commitments are left free to influence the conduct of life. If the personal standpoint could be satisfactorily accommodated for each individual in this domain, it might be possible to neutralize any further claims made by those with advantages in favor of a basic structure under which they would fare better than they could under a strongly egalitarian system.

This division corresponds in part to the distinction mentioned earlier between agent-neutral and agent-relative values. Impartiality provides quintessentially agent-neutral reasons—reasons to want something independently of your point of view—but they have to compete with many agent-relative reasons, from self-interest to personal attachments and commitments. Ideally the moral division of labor would assign the bulk of agent-neutral values to be realized by background institutions, leaving us relatively free to pursue agent-relative values in our personal lives.[27]

The motivational problems connected with acceptance of a general social framework as legitimate are different from the motivational problems that arise for individuals acting within it. Both types of problems concern the participants and their attitudes, but the basis of general acceptance ought to be much more impersonal than the basis of everyday conduct and personal choice. What we need is an institutional structure which will evoke the requisite partition of motives, allowing everyone to be publicly egalitarian and privately partial.

The trouble is that this is a pipe dream. If we try to imagine actual institutions that would realize it, we encounter overwhelming problems—problems concerning the legal and the economic character of the necessary arrangements, and the political and economic motives necessary to sustain them.

On the legal side there are two options. One would be to "constitutionalize" socio-economic equality. The other would be to realize it through a legislative program enacted by the ordinary methods of democratic politics. In either case, the legal structure would have to interact with the economy in such a way that efficiency, variety, and creativity in production and distribution were not destroyed, and space for the pursuit of individual life was preserved. Describing these conditions in the abstract, I find it impossible to imagine a system that satisfies them—one operated by human beings rather than bees. The steamroller socialism which puts the economy under direct political control plainly will not do it. I do not offer my inability

---

27. Edmund Burke would not agree. Here is what he says on the question whether ecclesiastics of the Church of England should be legally required to expend a certain portion of Church revenue for charitable purposes: "It is better to cherish virtue and humanity, by leaving much to free will, even with some loss to the object, than to attempt to make men mere machines and instruments of political benevolence." *Reflections on the Revolution in France,* p. 91.

to imagine a solution as evidence that none is possible, but let me explain why it is so difficult to see how these conditions might be met.

The first option, constitutionalization, if it were possible, would provide the most effective embodiment of the idea of a moral division of labor between impersonal institutions and the personal lives of individuals. Unfortunately it depends on what is probably an unworkable analogy. It envisions a socioeconomic "constitution" commanding our impersonal allegiance—comparable to the constitution which defines basic legal and political rights and insulates them against the effects of personal and parochial interests which inevitably play a leading role in ordinary economic life and ordinary democratic politics. But a political-legal constitution can be embodied in a limited set of rules, difficult to apply only at the edges, which need to change only slowly over time. By contrast, how are we to imagine what an egalitarian socioeconomic constitution could consist in, assuming that it also includes democracy and substantial individual liberty? It is not a matter merely of guaranteeing to everyone certain specific and fairly well-defined rights. What institutions would express such a commitment, and how could they operate on the basis of a wide impersonal allegiance without becoming vulnerable to the more personal and partial motives that animate ordinary politics?

A nation might be able to give constitutional status, protected from revision by political majorities, to certain essential types of public provision, and this would be an important step toward equality. A prosperous society could guarantee everyone medical care, education, decent housing, unemployment insurance, child care allowances, retirement benefits, and even a minimum income. It is entirely imaginable, in other words, that one might constitutionalize the elimination of poverty by a limited set of provisions which the legislature and the executive would be legally required to satisfy by more specific programs. To put these things beyond the reach of ordinary political bargaining and the calculus of interests would not only be an enormous social

advance in itself, but might be a first step toward further progress in the direction of more comprehensive socioeconomic
equality. It is that more comprehensive goal which concerns me
here, however. While it may be possible to expand the range
of specific rights guaranteed to everyone beyond basic free-
doms and political and legal equality, to include a social minimum of the kind described, this would not by itself amount to
a strongly egalitarian system. And that larger goal seems to me
beyond the reach of constitionalization.

For certain types of equality—legal, civil, and political—the
device of constitutional limitations on majority rule has been a
remarkable success. Those constitutional limits may take the form
of pure conventions or traditions, or they may be written law,
but in either case their effectiveness depends on their being
sealed off from the influence of most human motives. In fact it
is concrete evidence of the reality of the division of standpoints
that persons living under a constitutional democracy like the
United States can give their allegiance to a system which pre-
vents them from doing things which they believe they might
choose to do if they were not so prevented. I shall have more
to say about this phenomenon when we discuss toleration. At
this point we may note that the protection, against political interference, of equality in certain limited but fundamental areas
has proven to be compatible with inequality in the successful
pursuit of conflicting aims through democratic politics in other
areas.

The institutions through which these constitutionally basic
equalities are guaranteed owe much of their strength to the
fact that their aims are limited. They inhibit the pursuit of conflicting individual goals only in special ways, so that everyone
can be secure in possession of a common status and inviolability. Even without calling on a broader impartiality, this is something that most of us by now will not grudge our fellow citizens—and we are helped by the thought that it may protect us
as well.

Admittedly the interpretation of such provisions can be difficult, and a matter of political controversy. There are genuine difficulties in translating the ideals of political equality or equal protection of the law or sexual equality, or freedom of expression and freedom of religion, into concrete realities—both in deciding what each of them really means and in bringing it about. But the more comprehensive the general good that a political system aims to realize, the more difficult it will be to insulate the pursuit of that good—particularly if it is conceived in egalitarian terms—from the contrary influences of democratic politics. Freedom of speech and religion, due process and the right to vote, and protection against racial, religious, and sex discrimination can be hard-wired into a democratic political system and enforced by an independent judiciary. As I have said, this range of basic guarantees might be extended to include a social minimum. But the bases of broader economic and social equality present a much more difficult problem.[28]

These matters cannot be put beyond the reach of political bargaining and economic motives. The political and economic choices which affect a society's socioeconomic character have to be made constantly, by individuals who, whether acting as voters or as economic agents, bring to those choices a strong element of personal motivation, even if an impersonal element is also present. This mixture of motives would have to change for a strongly egalitarian society to command the support of a diverse population under conditions of individual freedom. And the changes in political motivation would have to coexist with motives in the economic sphere which were compatible with continued productivity. As things are, democracy is the enemy of

---

28. The possibility of discovering judicially enforceable welfare rights or "minimum protection" under the U.S. Constitution has been explored by Frank Michelman. See "Foreword: On Protecting the Poor Through the Fourteenth Amendment" and "In Pursuit of Constitutional Welfare Rights: One View of Rawls' Theory of Justice." More radically (though without reference to the U.S. constitution), Joshua Cohen and Joel Rogers have advocated a "Principle of Democratic Legitimacy" which would include the requirement, not subject to majoritarian revision, that economic institutions satisfy the Rawlsian Difference Principle. See *On Democracy*, pp. 158–61.

comprehensive equality, once the poor cease to be a majority. The interests of the majority do not usually coincide with the interests of all, impartially weighed together, and they certainly do not coincide with the ideal of equality.

My suspicion is that a politically secure combination of equality with liberty and democracy would require a far greater transformation of human nature than there is reason either to expect or to require. It may be possible in close-knit communities of exceptional solidarity, probably produced by racial or religious kinship rather than by the motive of impartiality. For large, ethnically diverse societies like our own, I am pessimistic. Internationally, of course, the situation is much more hopeless.

The best argument against such pessimism is that the world has gradually and unsteadily moved forward in its rejection of deeply rooted social inequality, and that many goals which would have seemed utopian in former centuries, like the abolition of chattel slavery or the enfranchisement of women or the prohibition of child labor, are now accomplished facts. Perhaps such things must be achieved step by step, so that there is something right in the perception of the unattainability of the ideal by a direct leap from where we are now. It may be a psychological condition of progress that people should become accustomed to the last advance and take it as the natural order of things, before gradually coming to perceive that there is a further advance bearing certain analogies to it which it would not be morally consistent to reject: However hard one tries, one can't distinguish between the two on grounds which justify granting one but not the other.

We have recently seen the operation of this benign slippery slope in the expansion of the concept of equality of opportunity to include not only the removal of external obstacles but also the provision of positive support to help people toward an equal start in life. So if in the next fifty years we moved toward establishing a decent social minimum, this might provide the platform from which to take further steps toward a more comprehensive socioeconomic equality, commanding stable political support.

But that would require a radical change in the motivation of political behavior. At present self-interest is expected to play a major role in democratic politics, only modestly qualified by impartial concerns. It would be a drastic change if the personal interests of voters were to come to have only a minor influence on their behavior, and only a minor role in the appeals of politicians campaigning for election. A division between personal and impersonal motivation which confined the personal almost entirely to individual rather than public choice seems, from the vantage point of the present, an unattainable dream.

This may be just another of those illusions of unalterability which attach to well-entrenched social practices, and which have attached in the past to practices such as the subjection of women that turned out later not to be unalterable after all. I certainly hope so. But even if it should prove possible to carry the moral division of labor to a much higher stage, in which impartial standards become dominant in the political domain, there would remain a further problem to which I see no solution. Economic life cannot be disentangled from private choice and personal motivation, without disastrous consequences. And the operation of such motives in the economy seems bound to frustrate the pursuit of a comprehensive egalitarian ideal however great may be the political will to achieve it. This is the familiar problem of incentives.

It is a problem which arises for all types of economy, and which cannot be evaded by the old socialist strategy, now being abandoned wholesale, of making the economy an extension of the state. Going by contemporary evidence, the advantages of a significant private sector in the economy of a modern society are enormous, as measured by productivity, innovation, variety, and growth. The productive advantages of competitive market economies are due to the familiar acquisitive motives of individuals, which lead them to exert themselves most energetically to produce or supply what others need or want not from benevolence, but from the hope of reward and the fear of failure.

Individual motivation is presumably no different in a socialist economy, but without competition, the incentives to make an effort are less. The production manager will always be tempted to think, "Do people really need to have these shoes in seven different colors, or this ice cream in 28 flavors?" and save himself some trouble. The probable costs in quantity, quality, diversity, and efficiency of production of everything people want make it doubtful that this would be a better alternative, even from the standpoint of impartiality. There is perhaps *something* to be said for a system in which everyone can afford what is available, though it offers little variety and a low quality of goods and services—as against a system with a great wealth of desirable products, and many people who can't begin to afford most of them. But how many would be prepared to say that the first society is really better, if its minimum and average standards of living are significantly lower in absolute terms?

To overcome these disadvantages would require not just market socialism but competitive market socialism or in effect simulated capitalism—something no one has invented yet. There would have to be competing firms—multiple ice cream companies, shoe manufacturers, silicon chip manufacturers, grocery store chains, and so on—with the real possibility of being driven out of business and the real possibility of new entrants into the market (or else the markets would have to be open to foreign competitors, whether socialist or not). There would have to be competing banks trying to profit from investment in entrepreneurial expansion.

All this might engage the egos of managers even without economic rewards, but whether it could be operated by a central state authority rather than a decentralized civil society is very doubtful. The political authorities would have to exercise heroic restraint not to dictate the results and to concentrate on keeping the system competitive. Besides, competition is alien to the spirit of socialism because of its emphasis on winners and losers, and its willingness to countenance so much wasted effort in order to be able to choose the best and discard the rest. But only competition—for money or fame, or the recognition of achievement or pure excellence—can be relied on to tap the strongest motives and the most creative ideas.

It is psychologically difficult to realize a decent social ideal with real people, as opposed to the characters in utopian fiction. In political life they can sometimes be counted on to permit impersonal values to override personal aims. They can also accept the complete or nearly complete authority of special impersonal values in their fulfillment of a specific public function such as that of judge or soldier or tax auditor, with whose proper execution their self-respect is directly involved. But it does not belong to the socialized nature of modern man in general to be motivated by a concern for the good of all in most of his working, let alone private, life. Arrangements based on other motivational assumptions cannot be relied on, and the result is that the most successful economies are competitive and give rise to substantial inequalities, which inevitably get passed on from generation to generation.

I do not have a better alternative to offer, but even if we can think of no way out of it, this has to be regarded as a bad situation. What capitalism produces is wonderful, but one cannot be content that the only incentives capable of such variety and efficiency of production also generate large and inheritable inequalities in the conditions of life, which in turn generate demands for their political protection.

In some sense it seems that people *shouldn't* behave this selfishly as political and economic beings. But it is not easy to describe a way in which they *should* behave, which will support an egalitarian system. Many of the motives involved are in themselves unobjectionable, taken one at a time. It is fine for people to want things for themselves and their families, to work hard in exchange for material rewards and long-term security, and to try to lead agreeable lives. No ideal of equality can alter the fact that it is what people want that makes production a good thing, in spite of the familiar claptrap about how the desire for consumer goods is only the result of brainwashing by advertisers. Expenditures in a market economy are an extremely effec-

tive way of transmitting to producers and suppliers information about what people want and what ways of satisfying them
are most efficient, and of stimulating the invention of new won-
ders. The trouble is that there seems to be no way of harness-
ing all this to a strongly egalitarian system.

How could a more equitable system work? As I have said,
one cannot look for guidance to the mode of operation of those
parts of a democratic political system which do succeed more
or less in supplying certain goods equally to everyone. Due process of law and the right to vote are not like shoes and food
and movies. Equality in the basic political and legal goods means
supplying everyone with the *same* thing. There is, to be sure,
the problem of supplying enough for everyone—making the
courts or the voting machines efficient and approachable enough
so that no one is denied access. But essentially the task can be
carried out by creating a procedure within which everyone is
treated the same by functionaries whose impartiality is subject
to public scrutiny.

This form can be reproduced in a system of rationing neces-
sitated by severe scarcity, when production cannot be increased
because of lack of resources. But it is not suitable in the more
usual case where demand for a good can lead to increased production, and where equality is not, as it is with voting, an absolute requirement. The question is whether any system can be
imagined in which the aims of economic life would be largely
unchanged but the incentives leading to the most effective
achievement of those aims were not economic. One needn't be
much of a pessimist to doubt it. The substitution of some form
of purely psychic income, like points in a game, is a natural
idea, but clearly utopian at this point.[29]

If economic inequalities could be greatly reduced by a method
compatible with both democracy and the maintenance of productivity, we could have a truly decent society. The remaining

29. Such an imaginary possibility is explored in detail by Joseph H. Carens
in *Equality, Moral Incentives, and the Market: An Essay in Utopian Politico-Economic
Theory.*

social inequalities and inequalities of status corresponding to differences of education, professional success, and family connections would be much less damaging if not connected to money. Within such an egalitarian framework, individual freedom to use one's resources as one wished, to choose one's mode of life, one's work, and one's associations, and to develop and express one's personal values and opinions—all these things could provide ample scope for the personal standpoint. Life would not be taken over by impersonal demands, for these would be met primarily by the framework within which life was led. However this is so far a pure fantasy, since the framework must be constructed and sustained by the collective conduct of individuals, and no one has yet designed a system which meets these disparate conditions simultaneously.

The impersonal desire for equality meets severe obstacles from individual motivation at every step: in regard to the basic institutions to which individuals are willing to give their allegiance, in the process of democratic politics, and in the operation of the economy. These obstacles may be partly overcome, but in light of the division of the self, an ideal social order is beyond my imagination, at any rate. This is not just pessimism about the wickedness of human nature. I do not think people are bad to occupy these conflicting standpoints, and while some of the obstacles to equality which I have described are due to morally objectionable degrees of self-interest, many of them are not. As Hobbes said about his description of the war of all against all in the *Leviathan,* he did not "accuse man's nature in it." Of course there is plenty of wickedness in the world. But it may be a consequence of our nature and our circumstances that, even without being morally at fault, we cannot at present design a form of collective life that is morally acceptable. However, that should not stop us from trying, and I shall now explore some possible responses to the standoff described so far.

10

Equality and Motivation

I want to consider what transformations of motive might make possible the realization of a more egalitarian social ideal. Given the inextinguishable appeal of egalitarianism and its enormous failures, together with the political and economic upheavals which they generate, this is an unavoidable question. Such an ideal could be sustained only if it were pervasively internalized. While institutions must play an important role in creating social and economic equality, they cannot sustain it unless they come to express what enough people feel.

Transformations in the tolerance of inequality can occur. In the United States, during my lifetime, and in other Western countries, there has been such a change in attitudes toward overt racial and sexual discrimination. (The change with respect to religious discrimination began a bit earlier.) This change is not limited to greater outspokenness by the victims, but has come to include a broad sense among the potential beneficiaries of discrimination that such benefits are illegitimate. I hope I am not too optimistic in believing that most white males in North America or Western Europe today would feel uncomfortable about being awarded a job or admission to a professional school under a policy that excluded blacks or women, or held them to higher qualifications. Most potential beneficiaries of such discrimination do not want it reinstated and would not, if it occurred, simply count themselves fortunate to be on the winning side of the racial or sexual divide. They would feel that benefits gained in this way were tainted, even dishonorable. Formerly that was not generally true; the legal abolition of overt discrimination—practiced, enforced, or protected by the state—has had a deep mental effect, which gives the legal result stability.

It was not easy to overthrow racial and sexual discrimination, and that is in a way encouraging, for it shows that the strength of resistance to a change does not necessarily forecast the instability of the result. However, societies in which these reforms took place had for some time already had a bad conscience, particularly about racism, and there was a lot of hypocritical rhetoric in the air.

This is not true of social attitudes to economic inequality, except with regard to extreme poverty. Those who win out in the competitive economy or as a result of the inheritance of wealth and social position tend simply to count themselves lucky, or deserving—certainly not, in most cases, as the recipients of ill-gotten gains, or gains whose origins make them disreputable. More people in our culture may feel this queasiness about inherited benefits than about earned benefits resulting from their productivity, but most, I suspect, feel it strongly about neither. The way the chips fall in a competitive economy where equality of opportunity is not blocked by traditional forms of discrimination may seem illegitimate to the losers, but to the winners and potential winners, it generally does not. Those with highly marketable skills rarely feel that their earnings are tainted, or that the difference between their standard of living and that of the average unskilled laborer is dishonorable.

In part this may reflect a belief that there is external justification for those inequalities, but it also indicates that for the most part prevailing opinion finds nothing prima facie wrong with them. Their beneficiaries feel on the whole entitled to count themselves fortunate in the natural abilities and social and educational opportunities which, suitably employed, have resulted in competitive advantage, and consequent rewards. Others are less lucky, but that's life. By contrast, the corresponding attitude toward the advantages of membership in a dominant race or sex is no longer respectable.

The creation of stable egalitarian institutions in a developed economy would require a change in these attitudes. Perhaps changed institutions can bring about the change in attitudes or perhaps they cannot; at any rate they will not survive unless they do. Not only the victims but the beneficiaries of socioeconomic inequality would have to come to regard such benefits with suspicion. But what change of this sort is possible? The question cannot really be treated separately from a consideration of the institutions in which equality might be embodied. Still, I should like to address it first as a problem of moral psychology.

It is a question of moral psychology because the problem of integration among different levels of motivation is crucial. The pressure toward change deriving from the claim of impartiality is clearly there, but the task is to imagine a transformed moral sense which responds to this claim better without being impossible to live by. Unlike the case of a theoretical change of world view, any such transformation must keep the personal standpoint constantly in mind.

When a theoretical discovery contradicts the appearances we simply allow it to overrule them with regard to what is true, and there seems to be no difficulty in doing this, even when important practical decisions depend upon it. Deceptive appearances don't continue to demand our belief, unless we are superstitious. Personal desires, on the other hand, remain effective for the most part, and cannot be rendered inactive at will.

If a very well-established principle is invoked, a desire can be decisively sidelined, as when one sees the No Smoking sign and puts out one's cigarette. But this is the manifestation of a requirement that has already been internalized, and I am talking now about the process of expanding, perhaps greatly, the authority of impartial values. Even the authority of No Smoking signs depends on the existence of a convention that most people, smokers and nonsmokers alike, can live with. The construction of an expanded egalitarian sensibility is a much more involved task. I shall try to describe the moral situation as it appears now, and then go on to consider alternatives.

First of all, an egalitarian system would have to completely forget the idea, still popular in certain quarters, that the root of social injustice is exploitation—in the sense of a failure to reward people in accordance with their productive contribution or the true value of their labor. The defense of equality requires that rewards *not* depend on productive contribution, and in particular that some people receive much more of the social product than they contribute.

People's productive contributions are so unequal that the mere avoidance of exploitation would allow great inequalities of economic condition. I assume no one believes in the labor theory of value any more; but just for the record, it is clear that the value of a product is not a function of the amount of labor that went into it. It is the other way around: The value of someone's labor is a function of its contribution to the creation of a product, together with the value of the product. In a factory that manufactures telephones, for example, the subtraction of the designers of the telephones and the production process would cause the productive value of the labor of the factory workers to plummet, roughly, to what they could produce in a pre-industrial economy, whereas the subtraction of an equal number of laborers from the factory would reduce its productivity only slightly by slowing down the rate at which it could produce telephones.

Second, the pursuit of equality requires abandonment of the idea that there is a morally fundamental distinction, in regard to the socioeconomic framework which controls people's life prospects, between what the state does and what it merely allows. There are other areas of state action, impinging on individual rights, in which this distinction retains its moral significance, and of course it will continue to do so at the level of individual morality. But with regard to income, wealth, social position, health, education, and perhaps other things, it is essential that the society should be regarded by its members as responsible for how things are, if different feasible policies and institutions would result in their being different. And if the society is responsible, they are responsible through it, for it is their agent.

This is an extremely important issue, and one on which current community opinion is unclear. But I believe there is still significant attachment to the idea that certain aspects of the economic system are "natural," and do not have to be justified: Only when government interferes with them is it responsible for the results, and then the question of the justifiability of its policies can be raised. Libertarianism is a radical version of this view, but in less clear form it has considerable influence on more mainstream public opinion. Its decisive abandonment would be a major transformation of the common moral consciousness.

As I said in Chapter 8, the acceptance of a serious egalitarian ideal would have to appeal to a notion of negative responsibility, on the part of the society, for failing to arrange things differently in ways that it could. If it is possible for people to be economically rewarded more equally under another arrangement, then maintenance of a system which allows rewards to be proportional to productivity would have to be regarded as a social choice to permit rewards to depend substantially on differences in natural talent, education, and background. Noninterference requires justification as much as interference does: *Every* arrangement has to be justified by comparison with every other real possibility, and if egalitarian impartiality has a substantial role in justification of this kind, then significant arguments on the other side will be needed to defend arrangements which permit large inequalities to develop as a consequence of their unimpeded operation.

A laissez-faire system, despite its name, has no special status as a "natural" process for whose results government is not responsible. In deciding to enforce only the rights which make such a system possible, the state makes a choice, and if there is a viable alternative, then it has chosen an arrangement which rewards those with greater productive capacity (and their heirs) at the expense of those with less—not in the sense that the latter are being deprived of some of the value of their labor, but in the sense that they are being deprived of what they could have under an alternative arrangement. The state, and therefore its citizens, are responsible for this result.

The sense that benefits not provided, which could be provided, are being *withheld* from the poor, will seem unnatural only if one rejects the assumption of negative responsibility. Of course if a more equal arrangement is chosen, then it is just as true that benefits are being withheld from the better off, which they would otherwise receive. But in an egalitarian view, this withholding may be justified by the priority of needs of those worse off. Whether it is or not depends on the arguments in the other direction.

In this respect, as I have said, political theory is different from the ethics of individual conduct. There, negative responsibility is much less significant: In a decent society, an individual who devotes most of his energies to the pursuit of his own life is not plausibly accused of withholding from others all the benefits he might provide for them instead. But the society itself must consider all systems of allocation prima facie equally eligible, since it has no "life of its own" to lead, apart from the way it arranges the collective life of its members. In deciding among alternatives, the importance of letting individuals lead their own lives must be weighed along with egalitarian values. But if, even in light of all that, the distribution of rewards is too strongly proportional to the natural or social accidents of birth, then the society must be regarded as having chosen to permit the distribution of benefits on morally irrelevant grounds. There is no default position that doesn't have to be justified because it is not chosen. Any way in which the society arranges things, any system it enforces, from laissez-faire to socialism, represents a choice which must be justified by comparison with the other viable alternatives.

This contrasts with the Lockean view that government constitutes an interference in the natural moral relations between individuals, which should be allowed to continue unless they threaten to break down without institutional support. In the view I am expressing, the existence of a legal order backed by government coercion is not in question: The only question is what it should do, and preserving the conditions for individual moral relations is only one of the tasks it makes sense to assign to it. It represents the ideal of a collectively held point of view of its members, and this ideal includes an impartial egalitarian element.

So if a society permits some people to become much richer than others and to pass this wealth on to their children, that is what it is doing—in a sense that is what we are all doing—and we have to ask the question whether the alternative arrangements in which these kinds of inequality would be less would be still more objectionable in other ways.

Let me now move to a more detailed discussion of the change in attitudes toward the causes of inequality that would be needed to overcome the resistance to an egalitarian system. We can distinguish three sources of socioeconomic inequality (inequality, from now on), which raise questions of social justice and to which attitudes can easily be different, and a fourth which in itself is relatively unproblematic.

The first is intentional discrimination of the traditional kind: racial, sexual, religious, ethnic. The remedy for this is negative equality of opportunity, or positions open to qualifications (including acquired qualifications such as education).

The second is hereditary advantage both in the possession of resources and in access to the means of obtaining qualifications for open competitive positions. The remedy for this is not so clear, because so long as children grow up in families, they will inevitably benefit or suffer from the advantages or disadvantages of their parents, even if inheritance of property at death is considerably restricted. But some of the effects with respect to access to the kind of background and training which enhance qualifications can be softened by public support for child care, education, and the like. I shall call this *positive* equality of opportunity, to distinguish it from the negative equality of opportunity which results from the mere absence of discrimination. (Rawls calls it fair equality of opportunity, and describes it as the attempt to ensure that those with the same natural abilities will have the same chances in life.)

The third source is the variation in natural abilities themselves, or what Rawls calls the natural lottery. He proposes a quasi-remedy to this in the form of the difference principle, but let us leave the question of remedy aside for the moment.

Let me refer to these three sources of inequality respectively as *Discrimination, Class,* and *Talent.* It will be clear that I am indebted to Rawls's discussion of the relative merits of different interpretations of distributive justice for this division. In his classification the system of Natural Liberty (with careers open to abilities) blocks the effects of discrimination, the system of Liberal Equality (with fair equality of opportunity) counters the effects of discrimination and class, and the system of Democratic Equality (his candidate, with the difference principle) counters the effects of discrimination, class, and talent.[30] I am concerned here with the character and legitimacy of differences in our attitudes toward these three sources of inequality. Finally let me add to the catalogue, for completeness and for purposes of contrast, a fourth important source of inequality, somewhat different from the others, which without further explanation I shall call *Effort.*

This fourfold classification omits one important category of causes of inequality, namely those influences on a particular individual's life which do not result from the social structure and which are not the individual's responsibility. These are instances of bad *luck,* in the ordinary sense: such things as being killed or crippled by accident or disease (including genetic disease), becoming unemployed because one's employer goes out of business, losing one's home in a tornado, and so forth. What the state should do about such inequalities is certainly a con-

30. See *A Theory of Justice,* pp. 71–75.

cern of political theory, but I have not included a separate discussion of it. I believe the main issue from the standpoint of
social equality is how to deal with inequalities in the impact of
this sort of individual bad luck on persons in different socioeconomic classes.

Whatever the social structure, people's individual luck will
differ, often in ways that are not determined at birth. While
amelioration of severe disadvantages of this kind should receive social priority directly, through medical benefits, assistance for the handicapped, and unemployment insurance, I believe variation in many of the more occasional forms of bad
luck should be incorporated into the definition of the life prospects or expectations of persons born into particular social positions with particular talents. If the resultant risks are much
higher for some groups than for others, that is obviously a
problem from the standpoint of social equality. But the determination of how much risk of inequality from accidental causes
should be allowed *within* any social class seems to me a different
kind of problem—a problem of what risks are worth running
for what benefits, or what costs are worth paying for the reduction of risk.[31] This is an important question, but quite different
from the questions about inequality posed by class and talent—
even though they too are in a sense a matter of luck.

I realize that much more needs to be said in elaboration and
defense of this claim. It requires an account of when inequality

31. Thomas Schelling has some interesting things to say about this subject.
In particular he points out that against a background of economic inequality,
the provision at public expense of specific, untradable benefits like medical care
or airport safety may not accurately reflect their value to everyone. Because the
rich already have more money, hemodialysis is worth more in money terms to
them than to the poor; and given the risks of kidney failure, the public money
spent to provide hemodialysis to everyone who needs it, including the poor,
might satisfy poor people's preferences better if spent on housing, or dispensed
as cash. See *Choice and Consequence,* pp. 9–17 and 141–42.

On the other hand there may be reasons not to allow public provision simply
to follow the lead of individual preferences. There are things a society may
want to provide for everyone, even if some of the beneficiaries would reasonably prefer to have the money to use for other purposes.

in outcome can be morally dominated by equality in antecedent risk, and when it cannot. But I won't pursue the matter here, and will confine myself to the original list of discrimination, class, talent, and effort, because of their greater importance for political theory.

These four factors can vary independently, though they are often correlated in one way or another, and can also interact causally. Discrimination, class, and talent may influence effort; discrimination, talent, and effort in one generation may influence class in the next. And all of them have their effects on inequality only through the operation of an articulated social system which includes different positions or roles, with different opportunities, advantages, and disadvantages attached to them.

It is clear that effort will always make a difference, but the range of possible outcomes over which effort will determine the result, and the rough functional relation between effort and outcome, is fixed in advance for each person by the combined effects of discrimination pro or con, the class into which he is born, his natural talents, and the existing social structure. Our judgment of the social structure will depend on our attitude toward the way it permits these causes of inequality to operate.

In the order given, the four causes form a natural progression, from external to internal. While all of them affect an individual's sense of who he is, they do not all originate with him.

Deliberate discrimination is a force completely outside the victim, imposed on him by others. Of course it is likely to have internal psychological effects which compound the resulting inequality; but in itself it is not a feature of the victim at all, but a fact about how others treat him.

Class is also environmental but is transmitted to the individual by his family, a kind of native socioeconomic habitat deriving from his most intimate personal relations in virtue of their relation to the rest of society. It is the product not primarily of deliberate imposition by outsiders, but of innumerable personal choices in a competitive economy of families, which constantly

generate stratification as a cumulative effect. Class can itself be
a target of deliberate discrimination as well, though when this
is systematic, with prohibitions on social mobility and intermar-
riage, it comes closer to a caste system. But even when it is a
pure by-product of the operation of an economic system which
permits social mobility, the class to which a person is born and
bred is entirely the result of causes external to him: He himself
contributes nothing to it.

Talent, as I am using the term, is innate, though its development and value depend on the other factors. (I shall usually
speak of *ability* when I wish to refer to realized talent.) It is
strongly internal to the individual, more an aspect of what he
is in himself than either discrimination or class, though of course
it generates material advantages only through his interaction
with others.

Effort, finally, being a manifestation of the will, is the most
personal or internal factor, and uniquely suitable to be regarded as the individual's personal responsibility.

The point was made earlier, in Chapter 7, that the egalitarian ideal is particularly concerned with equality in advantages
and disadvantages for which the recipients are not responsible.
In that discussion we were considering impartial concern in
general, and the egalitarian consequences of assigning priority
to the claims of the worse off when comparing overall states of
affairs. Here the topic is somewhat different—the fairness or
unfairness of social inequalities due to causes of distinct kinds.
It is the development of such a sense of unfairness which provides the most effective support for equality as a social ideal.

The essence of this moral conception is equality of *treatment*
rather than impartial concern for well-being. It applies to inequalities generated by the social system, rather than to inequalities in general. A society that permits significant inequalities among its members, in advantages and disadvantages for
which they are not responsible, will be perceived as failing to
treat them equally: it distinguishes in its treatment of them along
morally arbitrary lines.

The standard of equal treatment is more demanding with respect to equality than mere preference to the worse off (the pure priority view, as Parfit calls it), for it finds something unfair even about inequalities that benefit the worst off. That does not mean that the objection to such unfairness cannot be overcome by countervailing factors, including such benefit. But it does mean that the inequality, even if it harms no one, counts as something bad in itself, in a way that cannot be analyzed in terms of the pure priority view.

The pure priority view applies more generally, and it makes no objection to inequality per se: Any advantage to the better off at no cost to the worse off is all to the good, even if it is due to causes for which the recipients are not responsible.[32] This seems to me the only correct view to take of inequalities that arise naturally. For example there can be no possible objection to some people's naturally enjoying immunity to certain diseases or perfect health or sunny dispositions, even though this makes them much better off than those who are constitutionally sickly or depressed. Better is simply better, in such cases, because no inequality of treatment is implied. But once social mechanisms enter into the causation of a benefit, its unequal distribution becomes a form of unequal treatment by the society of its members, and the sense of unfairness makes its appearance. Sometimes, I believe, this may provide a reason to reject a Pareto-superior alternative because the inequality it permits is too great to be outweighed by other advantages. Such a criterion might imply that some socioeconomic inequalities are unfair even though they satisfy the difference principle.[33]

32. For this reason it is not counted by Parfit as a truly egalitarian position. See *On Giving Priority to the Worse Off*.
33. I must register a doubt at this point—a doubt as to whether the sense of unfairness here described is really so independent of the pure priority view after all. The problem is that whenever an inequality results from the operation of the social system, it is a product of human acts and choices, sometimes a side effect of market choices, sometimes the result of deliberate preference for particular persons. And whenever something is produced by human actions rather than by natural causes, we have the sense that it need not have occurred if

Let us now consider the four factors listed above from this point of view. By the standard of responsibility it would seem that only the last, effort (to the extent that it is independent of the others), should be immune from suspicion as a legitimate cause of variation in social condition. Yet there is a tendency to treat the other three factors as morally different from one another as well, with discrimination being most objectionable and talent least. Let us consider why this is so.

Discrimination is clearly the worst in one way: It involves deliberate imposition of disadvantages on some by others—unequal treatment in a strong sense—whereas class and talent produce advantages and disadvantages through the normal operation of a competitive economy populated by participants with normal human sentiments. Still, class and talent are not the individual's responsibility, even though they are not other people's responsibility in the way that deliberate discrimination is. This gives us a three-way classification: (1) causes for which others are responsible (discrimination), (2) causes for which no one is specifically responsible, only "the system" (class and talent), and (3) causes for which the individual himself is responsible (effort).

Now it would be possible to take either of two clear-cut po-

---

those actions had been different—even if we can't say precisely what alternative actions would have avoided it, or whether that is what should have been done, all things considered. This suggests that when we find a socially caused inequality unfair in the sense I have explained, it may be because we are comparing it with unspecified alternatives, involving different actions and choices by the members of the society, which would have been better by the standards of the pure priority view. That is, even if no practically available alternative with less inequality would be better for the worst off than the one we are considering, we may have in the back of our minds the thought that if human beings were to behave differently, this would not be true, and the worst off could be still better off. If this diagnosis were correct, the sense of unfairness about social inequalities would turn out, after all, to be explained by an application of the pure priority view to a range of alternatives broader than that ordinarily considered in circumstances of political choice. Perhaps these obscure remarks will become somewhat clearer in light of the later discussion. For the present, however, I shall proceed as if there is a sense of unfairness that applies specifically to inequalities caused by social institutions.

sitions with respect to this classification: (a) that only the first sort of cause is morally objectionable, or (b) that only the third sort of cause is morally *un*objectionable. But either of these positions would mean taking causes of type (2) as morally similar, either all unobjectionable or all objectionable. Yet many people, rightly or wrongly, perceive a morally significant difference between inequalities in advantages due to class and inequalities in advantages due to talent. While neither is generally condemned, there is more uneasiness about the first than there is about the second.

This can be seen from some of the reactions to Rawls's position on the moral arbitrariness of the natural lottery. Some readers of *A Theory of Justice* who are in favor of fair equality of opportunity as a way of limiting the influence of class on life prospects will nevertheless draw the line at the difference principle, with its implied denial of the intrinsic legitimacy of advantages derived from the employment of marketable talents. This is not just a reaction to a work of philosophy, but the manifestation of a moral attitude common in modern societies, which shows up in standard liberal politics.

I think the personal-impersonal conflict can help us to understand the appeal of this contrast, and more generally to understand why the four causes are naturally seen as forming a progression, of increasing moral acceptability. The responsibility of the "victim" is not the only factor determining our response: The entire motivational situation is relevant.

Let me say something about class before going on to talent. Discrimination is the product of a bad motive, prejudice, and there is nothing to be said for it.[34] But class depends on the

34. If a group has been systematically discriminated against in the past, it may be necessary in rectifying the situation to exclude other forms of differential treatment of that group as well, even when they are not motivated by prejudice. For example it would be unacceptable on statistical grounds to use membership in such a group as a probabilistic indicator of lower qualification for certain positions—even though other types of statistically based criteria of no greater reliability are admissible in filling those positions. Other criteria with inordinate impact on the group may also be suspect. This is a complication

special interest people take in their relatives, especially their children. There is no possibility of abolishing this interest, and no sane person would wish to do so. The only real possibility, for those of egalitarian sympathies, is to limit its scope of operation and the magnitude of its consequences. So long as people come in families, the approach to fair equality of opportunity can only be partial. The psychological aspect of the problem is the usual one: What division between personal and impersonal motives can be accepted by normal and reasonable human beings, with the support of an appropriate institutional setting?

In civilized societies, the best-entrenched limitation on the exercise of family preference is the rule against nepotism in public and semi-public institutions. This is really part of the principle of negative equality of opportunity, for it prohibits a special form of discrimination in the filling of competitive positions—a form more personal than racial, religious, or sexual discrimination. Given the strength of the preferential motive which it inhibits, the rule against nepotism represents a considerable triumph of the impersonal over the personal where it is in force. And its stability requires a general vigilance and some sense among the possible beneficiaries of nepotism (both those who could get the jobs or benefits and those who could dispense them) that there is something disgraceful about advantages obtained in that way. Even this minimal restriction requires a powerful partition of motives, since the motive behind nepotism remains acceptable in other contexts. Those in positions of influence who refrain from handing out jobs to their relatives or from attempting to bribe others to provide such jobs still spend money on their children's education partly in order to give them a competitive advantage in the open competition for jobs and social position.

If we add to the prohibition of nepotism a public effort to

---

having to do less with the ending of discrimination than with the removal of its effects.

provide fair or positive equality of opportunity, the personal-impersonal division is moved over a few notches, but the division remains. The stability of such a system requires a general sense that large competitive advantages resulting from exclusive access to higher education, for example, due to the accident that one's parents were well-to-do, are somehow tainted. Here again while the resentment of the losers is important, the uneasiness of the winners plays an important role in generating enough support for an egalitarian policy to prevent political revolt against its costs to them.

Yet even if such persons support the public provision of education and health care for all, in order to ensure everyone a fair start in life and a chance to develop those abilities which qualify for access to desirable positions, they will not stop favoring their children in their more personal choices. If they have the resources, they will continue to offer whatever extra advantages they can, by paying for superior education, by direct cultural enrichment, and by various forms of financial support. While these things are good in themselves, they also aim to give the child a competitive edge. This motivational split defines a familiar modern liberal mentality. I realize it attracts a certain amount of scorn, but that is quite unwarranted, for it is simply another example of the partition of motives which pervades morality.

Public institutional support for positive equality of opportunity does not abolish inequalities due to class, because it does not abolish the operation of family preference in the personal sphere, but merely seeks to limit it to that sphere. Operating there, it inevitably continues to have broader social effects because public institutions alone do not determine opportunities. Stratification is enhanced by the tendency of persons to marry within their socioeconomic class, and it is not diminished by social mobility between classes from one generation to the next. Social mobility is compatible with great inequality and it does nothing for those who stay put.

Any attempt to go beyond a certain point in eliminating the

effects of class so long as there *are* classes will run up against strong and natural human resistance, which will inevitably invade the political sphere. Attempts to redraw the personal-impersonal boundary through institutional redesign, by making privately purchased education illegal, for example, are likely to generate fierce opposition. This is a controversial issue, but I do not think such resistance can be simply discounted. It would stem not only from concern over the waste of possibilities, but from the feeling that a legitimate expression of familial preference was being blocked—that this was not like the rule against nepotism.

In short, even the standard forms of remedy to class-caused inequalities do not depend on the position that all inequalities due to class are morally unacceptable. A personal core remains protected, and this core has large social consequences, though its scope remains a matter for argument and institutional definition. Only a totalitarian government could even attempt to abolish classes, and even then it would be unlikely to succeed.

It would not be unrealistic to hope for a change in attitude toward the inheritance of wealth, so that the privilege of endowing one's children with independent means was no longer regarded as the kind of expression of family feeling with which the state should not interfere. It might even be possible to design a system of estate and gift taxes without the loopholes that usually plague such efforts. It would be a big change, but not unthinkable, if people ceased to regard it as a reason for someone to be rich that his parents were rich. But this would not make a serious dent in the effects of class, because differences in parental income and personally acquired wealth are enough by themselves to generate large competitive distinctions among children prior to the time that inheritance becomes an issue. So long as there are substantial inequalities in income there will be substantial inequalities due to class, barring some unimaginable evaporation or pathological inhibition of natural family sentiment.

A major cause of inequalities in income is variation in talent, and there we see the problem of how to draw the personal-impersonal division in an even more acute form. For some reason it appears to be harder to internalize the sense that advantages derived from the exercise of talent are in themselves morally suspect, on the ground that the talent itself is a matter of luck. Lucky or not, it seems too intimate an aspect of the individual, too tied up with the pursuit of life itself, for this attitude to sit comfortably. The fact that differences in talent are not themselves socially created may also play a role. This resistance seems to me unreasonable, but it is certainly there. Perhaps because everyone can imagine having been switched in the cradle, it is easy to think, about the members of a deprived class, "There but for the grace of God go I." But one's natural talents are not so easily switched, and that hinders the moral imagination.

It is true, of course, that your talents are an intimate part of you, and that any attempt by the state to prevent you from exercising and developing them would be intolerable. Like beauty, talent and excellence also attract recognition, admiration, and gratitude, and such responses are among the natural rewards of human life. But the economic rewards which some talents are able to command, if properly developed, are another story. They cannot be said to be merited just because the recognition of excellence on which they are based is merited. To try to sever the connection between talent and admiration would be wrong. But to sever the connection between talent and income, if it could be done, would be fine. Those with useful talents do not naturally deserve more material benefits than those who lack them.[35]

The problem would be different if there were an institutional vehicle, as we have seen for other causes of inequality, to

35. Could income be construed as the "natural" reward of certain talents—talents to produce what others are happy to pay for? It is a nice question, but I don't think so. The concept of a natural reward should be restricted to those advantages that are strictly inseparable from the recognition and appreciation of a quality by others, and I doubt that this is ever true of money. People's willingness to pay for something is a direct manifestation of their valuing it. But it needn't take the form of payment to the producer.

limit the effects of talent to a personal domain while blocking its consequences in a more public institutional setting which could then be governed by egalitarian principles. But that is just what is impossible for this case, unlike the case of class. One cannot realistically block the direct employment of talent to gain advantages in the public or semi-public sphere, as one can block nepotism and bribery. To do that one would have to abolish competition. Measures to block the influence of discrimination and class, by contrast, expand competition. In fact the aim of profiting from the exercise of talent is of utmost importance in the public sphere, and needs encouragement, not discouragement.

The advantages due to talent are not handed out as a reward for high scores on tests: They come as the result of demand for scarce resources in a competitive labor market. And the preservation of some form of labor market, with economic incentives, seems indispensible enough to provide an "external" justification for the differential rewards it generates. But if it is in operation, then people have to work for those rewards, employing their talents where the market reveals they are most in demand, and realizing economic and social gains when they succeed. The lives of people who work are pervaded by attempts to profit from their abilities in this way. I do not mean here to invoke the spectre of that mythical creature, rational economic man.[36] We all know that other motives are essential for the success of cooperative enterprises and that the exercise of a productive skill can itself be a source of real satisfaction. But economic incentives that generate inequalities also play a very significant role.

Any attempt to limit the inequalities due to talent without abolishing the labor market must take the indirect form of progressive and redistributive taxation. But this is quite different from limiting the effects of talent to a special, personal domain.

36. See Amartya Sen, "Rational Fools: A Critique of the Behavioral Foundations of Economic Theory."

Work is acutely personal, as well as public. So the motives of personal advancement and impersonal egalitarianism come into conflict very directly here. An egalitarian in a competitive economy is expected to strive for precisely those advantages which he simultaneously wants to limit.

If we follow the pattern of discrimination and class, wide support for an egalitarian policy with regard to talent would require that those who can profit from superior talent through the economic system should come to feel that such advantages are tainted, even though it is recognized that they must be allowed for reasons of efficiency. But with what coherent set of attitudes are egalitarians supposed to embrace these motives simultaneously? As acquisitive individuals they must force their socially conscientious selves to permit talent-dependent rewards as the unavoidable price of productivity, efficiency, and growth. As participants in the system they are expected, indeed encouraged, to pursue those advantages, but as citizens they are expected to allow them only reluctantly: They must regard it as legitimate and natural to want them, but in another light not legitimate to have them.

There is an analogy here with the case of nepotism, whose prohibition in the public sphere can coexist with family partiality in the private sphere; but the tensions involved in a partition of motives are in this case much more severe, and present more serious obstacles to equality. With regard to family connections it is possible, in theory at least, to approach a condition in which the institutions of the society are strictly egalitarian— through measures of positive equality of opportunity. But with regard to marketable talent, no such solution is available. The egalitarianism of the institutions is hostage to the anti-egalitarian partiality of the individuals out of which they are constructed.

The personal motives which lead people to develop and exploit their talents will dictate the degrees of inequality in reward that are required to satisfy even a strongly egalitarian standard such as the difference principle. The difference principle permits only those inequalities that benefit the worst off, but it can be applied only against the background of patterns of human interaction and motivation that determine which inequalities pass this test. Social institutions like the tax and transfer system will have to defer to these personal motives at every point, making the public domain an active participant in the generation of inequalities. So long as private motives remain significantly acquisitive and strongly partial, it is impossible to create a strongly egalitarian system without unacceptable invasions of personal freedom and disastrous economic consequences. The personal strictly limits what the impersonal can achieve.

The motivational problem for committed egalitarians in all this is that the egalitarian sense of fairness must make us regard as unfortunate those very inequalities which as economic actors we are bent on getting the benefit of, which our acquisitive demands make necessary, and which therefore are required for the benefit of the worse off. An economically competitive egalitarian with the appropriate partition of motives is supposed to reflect, as he signs the astronomical check for his three-star meal, that although it's a shame that business talent such as his should command such rewards while others are scraping by, there is no help for it, since he and his peers have to be allowed to earn this kind of money if the economy is to function properly. A most unfortunate situation, really, but how lucky for him!

The motivational situation would be less peculiar if an egalitarian system were imposed from outside, and personal acquisitive motives were free to operate within it. But if the maintenance of any such system is a political choice, which the participants are expected to accept, they will have to juggle two conflicting attitudes toward their competitive gains and losses, trying to maximize their take from what they regard as a morally questionable source.

There are really two problems here, one having to do with incentives in the operation of an ostensibly egalitarian system, the other having to do with its stability and political support. The first problem is that the application of any serious egalitarian standard, such as the difference principle, involves a choice among different *unequal* systems, and the available options will be determined not only by technological and material facts, but by motivational ones. So long as personal motives are permitted to determine individual economic choices, the inequalities that the difference principle must tolerate will be determined by fundamentally anti-egalitarian factors.

The second problem is that it is difficult to combine, in a morally coherent outlook, the attitude toward inequalities due to talent which generates support for an egalitarian system with the attitude toward the employment of their own talents appropriate for individuals operating within it. The first attitude is that such inequalities are unfair and morally suspect, whereas the second attitude is that one is entitled to try to get as much out of the system as one can.

While such a division of motives is not self-contradictory, it is not strictly intelligible. The essential problem is that while we know roughly what is appealing in the way of political and personal ideals, we cannot devise a political morality and a personal morality that fit together satisfactorily. The two pull in opposite directions because they respond to different demands, and the conflicts are too direct to be solved through a division of labor between social institutions and individual conduct. So the combination of egalitarian public values and inegalitarian personal aims to which we are forced by motivational logic simply lacks the character of an integrated moral outlook. The egalitarian sentiment of unfairness will tend to clash with the sense of entitlement to pursue one's own aims, and the acquisitiveness licensed by the latter will tend to erode support for the egalitarian system at the political level among those with higher earning power.[37] It is not like the case of people playing a fiercely competitive sport under strict rules—when support

37. This point is made by Mary Gibson in "Rationality," p. 219.

for the rules is guaranteed by the fact that without them winning is meaningless.

The strain of the division between internal and external views in this case is more severe than in the case of class, not because the motives deriving from the internal perspective are stronger, but because they are more pervasive. Life is shaped and controlled every day by the decisions about work and leisure, ambition and competition which drive an efficient system of production. There is no natural domain like that of family relations to which we can limit the operation of these motives, no natural division of the territory.

No such ambivalence surrounds the latitude given to inequalities resulting from differences of effort. They are not really inequalities in the same sense as those resulting from the other factors, since, as Ronald Dworkin has pointed out, decisions about how to allocate one's energies are more accurately regarded as an example of that freedom of choice among alternatives which is an essential element of equality. I believe that, apart from pathological conditions, the level of someone's effort is the result of free choice. Persons with the same resources and the same talents but different preferences will naturally choose to employ their talents differently, some taking their benefits in the form of more leisure, others in the form of this or that kind of commodity or opportunity or security. This enhances rather than disturbs the equality of morally significant advantages.[38]

38. See "What is Equality?" Parts I and II. In Dworkin's theory this is part of a broader claim that the appropriate metric of equality is resources rather than welfare—where resources are measured in terms of their cost to others, and what a person chooses to do with his time is not counted among his resources, even though the leisure of a productive individual may be quite costly to others. So if someone's tastes make it possible for him to be blissfully happy with only moderate resources, that is an inequality of benefit to which there is no objection. I find this plausible: The good fortune of such a person can be regarded as a natural blessing like perfect health, and so not unfair. Giving people the opportunity to determine the allocation of their own efforts, even if some prefer leisure to income and others the reverse, will likewise not of itself result in inequalities which are morally suspect. If the choices are voluntary, the base of equality of resources and options is morally dominant over inequalities in the consequences of such choices.

But the same freedom combined with differences in market value results in genuinely unequal advantages. There is no natural way to divide the causation of those advantages by talent into the legitimate and the illegitimate, along lines that could correspond to a psychologically plausible division between personal and impersonal motivation. All that can be done is to reduce the magnitude of the inequalities in life chances within which effort will determine the result. We cannot, as with class, distinguish those advantages that are inextricable from intimate personal choice and therefore immune from interference from those that are not: There is no analogue here to the distinction between legitimate devotion to one's children and nepotism. When it comes to work (as opposed to the diversions of private life), the use of abilities for our own advantage is both personal and public throughout. This helps, I think, to explain why inequalities due to ability arouse so much less opposition than inequalities due to class—even though the former inevitably give rise to the latter.

Also, it is impossible in practice to disentangle the effects of talent from the effects of effort, since effort is expended through the exercise of talent, and talent develops into a valuable ability only through effort. I don't mean that we can't distinguish the contributions of the two causes, only that we can't separate them. So if one does not object to inequalities due to effort, reluctance to prevent them will automatically carry over to the effects of talent that go with them.

To be sure, effort also combines inextricably with class in the causation of inequality: Those with privileged background and education, not to mention money, can profit more from a given effort than those with less. But we can at least try to compensate for that through measures of positive equality of opportunity, whereas nothing can be done to equalize natural abilities.

In light of these observations, the prospect of limiting social inequality to the goods for which their possessors are responsible seems remote.

11

Options

The general problem that emerges from the discussion of class and talent is this: There is a personal dimension of life in which egalitarian impartiality has no place, but which interacts with the public domain to generate inequalities that raise serious issues of social justice. Individual choices and efforts and personal attachments which are in themselves unexceptionable combine on a large scale and over time to produce effects that are beyond individual control and grossly unequal.

The dual sources of the inequalities compete for dominance in determining the appropriate moral response. On the one hand there is some temptation to say that since family sentiment and inequalities in talent are themselves not objectionable, but simply part of the way the world is, there is nothing either right or wrong about inequalities in benefit that derive from them in a social context. They do not require further positive justification (though it may be justifiable to eliminate or modify them for other reasons). On the other hand there is the sense that once natural differences combine with social institutions to generate inequalities, the results require moral justification in terms of the standards of justice appropriate to public institutions—in the natural-social mixture, the social is morally dominant, as it were.

This is essentially Rawls's view. It is the opposite in spirit to Locke's theory of the generation of property rights by the mixture of personally owned labor with common resources—a mixture in which Locke thought labor was morally dominant, generating ownership in the results. Rawls believes the contribution of the social system to the generation of these results is morally dominant, triggering a presumption against inequalities unless independently justified.

I share Rawls's egalitarian sentiments, and might even defend something more egalitarian than priority to the worse off, given the factor of social causation. The fact that we are not responsible for our talents renders morally questionable all but the most immediate inequalities that derive from them. But this poses the problem, and does not solve it. Individual motives remain, and they work against equality in two ways: by inhibiting support for institutions which attempt to reduce it, and by putting pressure even on institutions that give priority to the interests of the worse off to tolerate substantial inequalities as the price of efficiency. At the same time these motives seem to play an essential role in the successful operation of a modern competitive economy.

Altogether, the possibilities of change seem limited. The psychological difficulties of combining political egalitarianism with personal acquisitiveness are clear. But the substitution of other personal motives will not work either. People can of course be motivated to work hard at something they are interested in for its own sake, and sometimes this will yield a product which others also want. But it is a romantic fantasy to imagine the world run on such a basis. We cannot all be creative artists, research scientists, or professional athletes. It wouldn't even be enough if everyone was strongly motivated to do his job well. Each of the hundreds or thousands of parts that go into a washing machine or a truck or a ball-bearing factory has to be designed and manufactured by people motivated by economically expressed demand. They are not going to do it as a form of self-expression, and even if they wanted nothing better than to contribute to the well-being of mankind, this would not tell them what exactly to make in their semiconductor plant.

Benevolence is not enough. Even love of semiconductors is not enough. Among those who have to think of new things to

do and new and more efficient ways to do them, there seems
no substitute for the market as a source of information, and
the most effective motive for responding to that information is
a strong investment of personal ambition and desire for success
in productive activities that will pay off.[39] It is hard to do without people who work hard and exercise their ingenuity for gain
and competitive success; yet in a stable egalitarian society they
would have to combine this with a desire to live under a system
which made it as difficult as possible for them to achieve these
goals.

Some restrictions, because of their limited character, combine easily with an ethos of the pursuit of profit. The prevention of negative externalities, through the control of pollution
for example, can exclude certain means to economic advantage
without requiring a change in the basic motive. Admittedly we
find limited enthusiasm for such regulation from those whose
profits are reduced by it, but the point is that there is in principle no motivational difficulty about the partition of motives
which would permit support for such boundaries around the
domain of legitimate acquisitive activity. It is analogous to the
rule against nepotism, which limits the ways one can benefit
one's relatives, without requiring any basic change in the wish
to do so. Another example is anti-trust regulation, which estab-
lishes the framework for competition. An impersonal motive in
support of the framework can coexist with the personal motives

39. Cf. John Stuart Mill: "The verdict of experience, in the imperfect degree
of moral cultivation which mankind have yet reached, is that the motive of
conscience and that of credit and reputation, even when they are of some
strength, are, in the majority of cases, much stronger as restraining than as
impelling forces—are more to be depended on for preventing wrong, than for
calling forth the fullest energies in the pursuit of ordinary occupations. In the
case of most men the only inducement which has been found sufficiently constant and unflagging to overcome the ever-present influence of indolence and
love of ease, and induce men to apply themselves unrelaxingly to work for the
most part in itself dull and unexciting, is the prospect of bettering their own
economic condition and that of their family; and the closer the connection of
every increase of exertion with a corresponding increase of its fruits, the more
powerful is this motive." *Chapters on Socialism,* p. 263.

of gain that operate within it, and that would, if left to themselves, lead to violations of the framework. The sense of the participants' common interest in establishing such rules also plays a role in these cases.

Acquisitiveness is motivationally compatible with the desire to provide at public expense a social minimum of some kind, for those who lose out badly in the competitive economy. This might be set at various levels, depending on the wealth of the society. But a decent social minimum is very different from an egalitarian policy. It does not require for its support a general suspicion of inequalities due to class or talent—all it requires is the sense that there are certain things no one should have to suffer through no fault of his own, if they can be prevented without too much cost. Here again the necessary partition of motives is clearly feasible, with acquisitiveness proceeding within a system of moderately redistributive taxation.

The trouble with stronger forms of egalitarianism, from a motivational point of view, is that they require too exclusive a reliance on egalitarian impartiality for support of the economic framework, and too complete an insulation of politics from personal motives. They require some as yet unimagined change either in the motivation of economic actors or in the design of economic systems, or both, which will support the incentives and generate the information needed for productive efficiency without at the same time generating large inequalities. The upshot of the discussion so far is that even if the principle of negative responsibility is widely accepted as regards the society's relation to the life chances conferred by its socioeconomic structure, there are serious obstacles to the additional changes in the pattern of personal and interpersonal motives which would be needed both to generate unanimous support by reasonable persons for a system which tried radically to reduce inequalities due to class and talent—and to make such a system work. If all this is true, then those who are attached to egalitarian ideals seem to be left with two options. Either they can lower their sights and aim for a partial approach to those ideals, through changes falling within the limits imposed by the present general character of human motives and the consequences of their interaction. Or they can hope for a more radical transformation of attitudes which, together with institutional changes, would lead to a much fuller realization of socio-economic equality, while nevertheless leaving a personal sphere free for the expression of a reconstituted individuality.

The first option, a plainly nonutopian possibility which has considerable appeal in its own right and which is a natural fallback position from strong egalitarianism, would be a development of the already existing uneasiness about severe poverty in relatively wealthy societies into a much stronger insistence on a high social minimum, with healthy, comfortable, decent conditions of life and self-respect for everyone. This would be in addition to fair equality of opportunity, so that even those unable to command good incomes in a competitive economy would be guaranteed a decent standard of living.

Such an attitude need not be linked to any discomfort about inequalities above this level. Of course the social minimum would have to be financed by progressive taxation, used to support social services and a negative income tax (which would most effectively express the underlying idea if it were automatically added to wages just as positive income tax is automatically withheld from wages). This would have the effect of reducing the spread of disposable income above the social minimum; but the change of attitude I am imagining would not include a desire for such reduction for its own sake. And it would also, most importantly, not include any uneasiness of conscience on the part of those who are far above the social minimum. Essentially it would abandon the idea of unfairness according to which all socially generated inequalities are suspect unless vindicated by a suitable condition of responsibility. Provided the minimum is set sufficiently high, individuals with competitive advantages would have no reluctance to pursue and enjoy affluence for themselves and their families. Therefore this attitude would do nothing to damp down the acquisitive motives that drive a competitive economy. There would be the task of designing social provision and a negative income tax so as not to destroy incentives among those being subsidized up to the social minimum; but that problem should be soluble. So long as it is possible to maintain a significant positive correlation between work and income, a guaranteed base will not prevent most people from working, since most people want more than they have.

This is essentially the point of view behind contemporary social democracy, which has never been politically significant in the United states, and seems to be in retreat in Europe, but which may have a future. If such an attitude became entrenched in a modern society, it would not support an egalitarian system and would not hinder the formation of classes, nor would it support unqualified application of the difference principle, since the priority of gains to the worse off would cease once they reached the social minimum. But it would mean that the society put every effort into combating the worst aspects of inequality—poverty and severe relative deprivation. While it would imply a rejection of the idea that those with competitive advantages were not entitled thereby to gain economically, it would likewise reject the idea that all anyone was entitled to was what he could command in the labor market. Something like the right of everyone to a decent standard of living, provided this is economically feasible, would be accorded priority in the economic organization of the society.

This is hardly an unworthy goal, and it may be that nothing beyond it can be seriously pursued until this much has been achieved and has become so well entrenched that it is considered the natural order of things: Then it will be time to complain that it is not yet good enough. But those who hope for something more in the long run must consider the second option—a psychological and institutional transformation which would permit innovation and cooperative production without generating substantial inequalities of reward.

In relation to the present state of things this is unavoidably an exercise of utopian imagination; but the change of attitude that suggests itself, one which would be far more egalitarian and more in line with the traditional ideals of socialism, is the development of a general reluctance on the part of members of the society to be conspicuously better off than others, either in standard of living as measured by consumption or in social advantages—and a corresponding disapproval of those who try to make themselves significantly better off in these ways. The reluctance would have to extend to special advantages for one's family as well.

This would not mean a takeover of all motives by the impersonal standpoint. Impartiality and egalitarianism would apply to the social structure, but not to private life, and individuals would be expected to devote their energies and their personal resources to the pursuit of happiness and the benefit of their families. But they would not be strongly motivated to get ahead of others—in fact the reverse: Their concern would be to reduce gaps between others and themselves, wherever in the socioeconomic spectrum they found themselves. If they were near the bottom, moving ahead would be the goal; if they were near the top, they would want less, and more for others. What I am imagining is not a general outbreak of asceticism. People would still want material comforts, good food, and vacations in Italy; but they would not feel right about having these things if other members of their society could not afford them.

It may be thought that this change is psychologically too bizarre to be worth considering, but I do not think it is out of the question. It might conceivably come about as the result of a long development, in which the attachment to equality extended to wider and wider areas of life, producing an intergenerational shift in people's sense of what they were entitled to, which would reduce resistance. But I grant that such a thing is highly unlikely, even over the very long run.

Apart from the issue of its psychological possibility, however, this change would not be enough by itself to create egalitarian prosperity. Something else would have to happen to fill the gap in incentives to economic activity that would open up if economic competitiveness disappeared from the scene. The desire to have more, but not more than others, seems very difficult to harness as an incentive for productive effort. If the acquisitive impulse disappears among those with the strongest potential competitive advantages, other incentives must replace it or else a market economy will slow down, cease to innovate, and cease to improve its per capita productivity, on which everyone's welfare depends.

Other incentives are possible, at least in some segments of the work force. Peer approval and derision provide very strong competitive incentives in professions in which the "jury" is well defined and the quality of performance is easy to determine. This presents the problem of seeing to it that approval attaches to what really matters. In the academy, the only case with which I am personally acquainted, the "reputation" incentive to engage in research is considerably stronger than the incentive to teach well; still, the appreciation or boredom of students carries weight with some of us. And in uncorrupt countries, civil servants including the military have to be motivated to do their jobs well on noneconomic grounds, more or less.

Perhaps such motives could do much of the work of economic incentives in some professions, and in addition the leveling attitude would prevent the upward pressure on salaries that results from competition for scarce talent. But what about the main productive elements of the economy? It is hard to imagine what could replace economic incentives in the determination of decisions about how to stock a hardware or grocery or clothing store, what colors and kinds of paint to manufacture, or how much to charge for a silicon chip. Success in the economy cannot be identified independently of economic success—at least the economic success of the enterprise in which one is engaged. Profitability is a condition of capital accumulation and increased production, so even if volume and numbers of satisfied customers are the standard of real success, economic gain must be the primary influence on decisions in the business world.

A natural proposal is to try to detach the informational function of markets and profit-maximization from the motive of
personal gain—with other, purely moral incentives substituted
that follow roughly the same contours of penalty and reward.
This would require either a finely graded system of public recognition of economic performance—market socialism with
medals and honor rolls—or a change in the basis of most people's self-esteem which made it possible to run the whole system
on Monopoly money, which they would be proud to earn even
if they couldn't spend it on themselves.

Neither of these scenarios is particularly credible. I think it
much more likely that the general settling in of an aversion to
consuming more than others would undermine competitiveness generally in most of the economy, and leave it strong only
in the arts and sciences, in sports and entertainment, and in
those professions which offer the possibility of fame, at least in
the eyes of a special audience. Perhaps there is some alternative
method of using straightforward economic incentives in such a
way that large economic inequalities do not develop from their
operation; but no one has yet dreamed up such a system, and
it would seem to require an unimaginable level of information
and control by the authority that determines what the incentives will be.

My conclusion, as before, is that a strongly egalitarian society
populated by reasonably normal people is difficult to imagine
and in any case psychologically and politically out of reach, and
that a more real possibility lies in the first alternative. Intolerance of severe poverty at least receives lip service in most liberal societies, and it ought to be possible to develop it into insistence on a higher and higher social minimum, until it becomes
intolerable in a rich society if anyone does not have a decent
standard of living and a fair opportunity to go as far as his
natural talents will take him above that.

Even this would be an extraordinary transformation, but it
would be compatible with great inequalities and a strong class
structure which the absence of obstacles to social mobility would

do nothing to destroy. I therefore think it is not a result we can be content with. Rather, it illustrates the difficulty of bringing together personal and impersonal standpoints and encourages the belief that an acceptable combination of individual and political morality remains to be invented.

12

Inequality

Having expressed so much regret over the difficulty of moving closer through politics to equality of socio-economic condition, I may have given the impression of hostility to inequality of any sort. It is now time to counter that impression.

Even if people's lives are equally valuable and important from the standpoint of political theory, many other things are not. Unfortunately it is not always easy to prevent egalitarianism in political morality from infecting other values. If one is really uneasy about socioeconomic stratification, one can become uneasy about cultural, educational, and aesthetic stratification as well. That is particularly likely where the agency of the state is involved. And even if one sees the need to treat different goods differently, there is a genuine problem of reconciling legitimate egalitarianism with the recognition of qualitative rank and excellence, since the provision of greater public support to art or research deemed valuable in itself is automatically also a selective benefit to those individuals who care about it, appreciate it, or engage in it.

Mill's distinction between higher and lower pleasures is one attempt to combine an assertion of the equal value of persons with an unequal evaluation of what they care about, through the assignment of unequal value to different forms of enjoyment. But this renders purely formal the equal value of persons capable of the higher pleasures and those capable only of the lower. The lives of the latter simply contribute less to the general good so they are less important from a utilitarian standpoint: Their getting what they want *counts* less, in virtue of their tastes. This is brought home by the explicit analogy with the lesser importance of the experiences of animals in Mill's discussion.[40]

I prefer a clear distinction between the value of experience and the value of its objects. Some things are in themselves more valuable than others, and this cannot be analyzed in terms of the greater value of their enjoyment. It may be that the enjoyment of what is better is more valuable than the equal enjoyment of what is worse, but that would be a *consequence* of the order of intrinsic value, not its basis. In any case it is a separable question, and I would not favor the use of such a standard in determining the relative moral weight of people's interests for distributive purposes.

None of this is incompatible with Mill's epistemological point that the only evidence we can have for the value of anything is what people want, or value, on reflection and in light of wide experience. People can be mistaken in such judgments, but in correcting such mistakes we must rely ultimately on the evidence of further desires. Nevertheless the evidence must not be confused with the thing itself: The value of something intrinsically valuable is not constituted by the value of the experiences of those who actually enjoy it. Such enjoyment is also valuable, but the value of the object is something distinct.

Moral equality, the equal primary importance of everyone's life, does not mean that people are equal in any other respect. They are not, and a complex culture magnifies their inequality and diversity by permitting a wide range of achievement and the flourishing of different talents. So far as we are concerned with individuals, we should be concerned to further everyone's development in light of their natural abilities. But support for what is simply excellent cannot be based on a concern for individuals at all, either egalitarian or individualistic. It must draw on a different motive—a respect for what is valuable in itself.

40. *Utilitarianism*, chap. 2.

That is the appropriate attitude toward great artistic and intellectual creations, as well as toward the beauties of the natural world. To justify their support or preservation in terms of their value to individuals is to get things backwards.

To acknowledge such values and give them an important role in political justification introduces a tendency which is strongly anti-egalitarian in its effects, simply because people are so unequal in their creative and appreciative capacities. It is a function not only of ability but of class, since so much education and culture is transmitted informally through the family, and much of the motivation which directs individuals toward higher pursuits is also due to family influence. So a society which supports creative achievement and encourages maximum levels of excellence will have to accept and exploit stratification and hierarchy. The educational system and the system of support for science, scholarship, and the arts will have to include a frankly inegalitarian element, even if its broad base is geared to providing fair equality of opportunity, perhaps supplemented by compensatory assistance for those of least ability.

Some of the justification for the support of excellence is instrumental, since many original discoveries or creations eventually benefit everyone, and others—great works of architecture, for example—are important public goods. The support by an egalitarian democracy of a selective system of education and research can be defended effectively in such terms. But I believe the argument should not be restricted to this form. Beauty and understanding are valuable even if they are appreciated only by a minority, and a society that does not recognize this is impoverished.

There are problems about intrinsic value that I can't take up here. For example, while the value of something beautiful is not a function of the number of people who can enjoy it, if *no one* can ever enjoy it the value of its existence seems to vanish. If the entire human race went permanently blind, the destruction of the paintings in the Louvre would not be a further loss. But so long as there is one person to look at them, their destruction would be a catastrophe. Perhaps the value (though not the quality) of works of art depends on their being perceivable.

But without having a theory about it, I wish to claim that there are values which are not just the values things have for persons, and that such values provide legitimate goals for a society. By calling these goals legitimate I mean that reasonable persons ought to agree that the resources of the state which they support and which represents them should be used to further such ends, as well as to protect and benefit equitably all the members of the society. It is a legitimate form of collective action through the agency of the state.

This position introduces an element into political theory which is controversial, and which is allied to perfectionism. In the section of *A Theory of Justice* called "The Principle of Perfection," Rawls rejects perfectionist goals for the basic framework of society, on the ground that they necessarily import particular conceptions of the good which are disputed in a pluralistic culture, and that the society has to be fair among the parties to such disputes. On this view, it should avoid assuming the correctness of any one conception of the good in determining its basic structure and goals, because this could not command the acceptance of all reasonable members. The suitable method for pursuing perfectionist goals in a just society is through the voluntary association of those attached to them:

> While justice as fairness allows that in a well-ordered society the values of excellence are recognized, the human perfections are to be pursued within the limits of the principle of free association. Persons join together to further their cultural and artistic interests in the same way that they form religious communities. (pp. 328–29)

and:

> The principles of justice do not permit subsidizing universities and institutes, or opera and the theater, on the grounds that these institutions are intrinsically valuable, and that those who

engage in them are to be supported even at some significant
expense to others who do not receive compensating benefits.
Taxation for these purposes can be justified only as promoting
directly or indirectly the social conditions that secure the equal
liberties and as advancing in an appropriate way the long-term
interests of the least advantaged. (p. 332)

He does admit another possibility of supporting such goods
by taxation, but only through a special mechanism which he
calls the "exchange branch." This is a special representative body
which, against the background of a just distribution of income
and wealth, can authorize government activities independently
of what justice requires, but only under the condition that "no
public expenditures are voted upon unless at the same time the
means of covering their costs are agreed upon, if not unanimously, then approximately so" (p. 282). The idea is that no
one should be taxed for such purposes without his consent.

I think this goes too far, even though I agree that fairness
among the parties to basic disputes over the nature of the good
is an essential aspect of justice, crucial in the defense of toleration. That there are things good in themselves, however, seems
to me a position on which reasonable persons can be expected
to agree, even if they do not agree about what those things are.
And acceptance of that position is enough to justify ordinary
tax support for a society's effort to identify and promote such
goods, if it can effectively do so—provided it does not engage
in repression or intolerance of those who would have chosen
different candidates.

The effort is legitimate even if mistakes are made, because
the promotion of what is excellent is, under that description, a
valid collective goal even for an involuntary association like the
state. This does not mean that the majority has a right to take
over the power of the state for its private purposes; rather,
everyone has reason to want the state to identify and encourage
excellence, and this will require a method of selection which
will inevitably leave some people unsatisfied with the result, even
though they can accept the aim.

In a democratic society, such values will be publicly promoted only if they are generally acknowledged, even by those who are not personally interested in fine art, fundamental research, or natural wilderness. There has to be a general willingness to accept the judgment of experts in deciding what to support—but such willingness is not unknown in democratic societies. Most important, the inequalities in public expenditure required for such support have to be considered acceptable—not because those who are creative or capable of appreciating the best deserve more, or because their pleasures are higher and should count more heavily in calculating the general welfare, but because they are effective instruments toward the creation of some of the best things in the world. We thus support through the society certain values that we cannot advance equally as individuals.

In this respect I believe a good society should be anti-egalitarian, and committed to developing the maximum levels of excellence possible—a mildly Nietzschean note. It is also essential to maximize access, but that will not promote equality, only mobility. In particular the tendency toward equality and distrust of the exceptional found in the public educational systems of some modern liberal societies is a great mistake. Equality of opportunity is fine, but if a school system also tries to iron out distinctions, the waste from failure to exploit talent to the fullest is inexcusable. It also undermines equality of opportunity, so long as there are private schools to which children of the upper classes can escape to get a high-powered education if they have the ability, while the lower classes are mired in mediocrity whatever their talent. The position I favor is maximalist. A society should try to foster the creation and preservation of what is best, or as good as it possibly can be, and this is just as important as the widespread dissemination of what is merely good enough. Such an aim can be pursued only by recognizing and exploiting the natural inequalities between persons, encouraging specialization and distinction of levels in education, and accepting the variation in accomplishment which results.

The recognition and exploitation of human diversity and inequality of talent would present fewer difficulties if it were not so strongly connected with economic inequality. But at least one might hope that creative and scholarly activities could serve largely as their own reward, under a more egalitarian system of compensation. What cannot be done is to separate the pursuit of excellence from the creation of inequalities of status, and it must be acknowledged that such inequalities can cause a good deal of pain. It is some consolation that the pain will often be felt by those who have chosen to compete in the relevant arenas of achievement—unlike the effects of class status, which never depend on choice. Many of the competitions of life are not ours to choose, however, and there would be an ineliminable cost in self-esteem to those who achieve less than others even in a society without marked economic inequalities. But in the end, the unhappiness of unsuccessful contenders, or the low self-esteem of those who cannot even make the attempt, are not evils that a decent society should be asked to weigh in the balance against the concentrated support of what is best. Such inequalities are inextricable from the recognition and pursuit of certain values too important to be compromised.

This brings me, however, to a final question which poses a threat to much of what I have said so far. I have focused so insistently on the problem of socioeconomic inequality, contrasting my objections to this with the desirability of accepting inequality of other kinds, that it is essential to say something about why art and science are so different from money.

Let me begin by putting the case on the other side: Why shouldn't it also be regarded as a good thing about a society that it permits some people to live in great economic freedom and luxury, even if their access to this possibility is largely a matter of luck? Naturally it would be best if everyone could live this way, just as it would be best if everyone could write wonderful poetry. But what if everyone cannot? If someone of independent means leads a life of great cultivation, refinement, and pleasure, why not regard that simply as a good in itself, untainted by the fact that such a life is not available to most people? The life of a gifted artist or musician or scientist is not available to most people either, and all such lives may require resources that could be shared more equally if they went to more mundane purposes.

In short, why not be a maximalist about pleasure and the things that money can buy? Suppose a society can guarantee all its members a decent social minimum. What is the objection to regarding anything any of them can get above this as another form of excellence in life, however morally arbitrary may be its causes? This could be asked about many of the goods that people with money spend it on. Why not be glad to see some individuals attain them to the greatest possible degree, whatever their causes and however unequally they are distributed—provided no one is excluded by discrimination from the opportunity to acquire these things?

If this question has an answer, it must depend on the judgment that a life of luxury and refinement is more accurately viewed as good for the person who leads it than as a good in itself. I am not sure that is entirely true, but it is largely true. A society and its rules constitute a collective enterprise, and the way it operates should be as nearly as possible acceptable to all its members. I believe that to produce or make possible what is best in itself, in various dimensions of excellence, is a reasonable social aim which can hope for wide support even if it means that some people will benefit from those goods much more than others. But when it comes to the generation of benefits for individuals considered as such, then so long as we accept the principle of negative responsibility for what the social structure allows, some form of egalitarian impartiality should be the dominant value.

It does not seem plausible to defend the wealth of a few in perfectionist terms drawn from the example of social support for the artistic or scientific or scholarly work of a few, or for the preservation of the natural order. These latter perfectionist goals are legitimate collective ends because their unequal benefit to individuals is incidental. But wealth is primarily a benefit to individuals, and therefore subject to egalitarian constraints. If someone rebuts an egalitarian complaint against an aristocratic ideal by saying that his fabulously expensive life is a work of art, we are entitled to be skeptical. Even if an expensive and cultivated style of life is a kind of aesthetic achievement, that cannot be its dominant characteristic from the collective point of view of political justice.

On the other hand it is not so easy to dismiss the pleasure many people derive from knowing and hearing about lives of luxury and taste led by others, at a level which is possible only for a few because of its cost. Even if some people find it unsavory, vicarious pleasure in contemplating the enjoyment by others of beautifully landscaped estates, grand houses, high fashion, exquisite furnishings, private art collections, and so on is an undeniable and widespread fact of life which has survived the disappearance of aristocratic societies. Some of the most wonderful things in the world just are rare: There is no way around it.

I suggest with suitable trepidation that this may justify a society in trying to adopt economic policies that permit such extremes. As things are, these luxuries are the concomitants of earned or inherited wealth. But even if inequalities of that kind could be radically reduced, it would be desirable to permit in some other way the enjoyment of life at its upper boundaries by a few. While there may be no ideal way to distribute such opportunities, I believe no egalitarianism can be right which would permit haute cuisine, haute couture, and exquisite houses to disappear just because not everyone can have them.

13

Rights

In contrast to the difficulties faced by the pursuit of equality, the protection for each individual of a sphere of personal autonomy is the object of a well-developed and effective tradition of ethical and institutional design. This tradition is accepted in only a minority of cultures, but where it is accepted it works very well, and its main resource is the definition and protection of individual rights.[41]

The individualist component in the perpetual opposition which shapes political theory comes from everyone's need to lead his own life, guided substantially by personal motives arising from his particular perspective and situation. The design of conditions of political association acceptable from this point of view requires certain well-defined degrees of freedom for individuals, knowable in advance, and not subject to limitation or interference except for exceptional causes, most of which are avoidable by the individual himself with sufficient care.

These are exclusive rights—rights which exclude others from directly interfering with their enjoyment or exercise—as opposed to the nonexclusive rights which Hobbes says everyone has to everything, "even to one another's body,"[42] in the state of nature. Two persons can both have the nonexclusive right to possess the same object: Neither of them does wrong if he

41. In this chapter I shall refer only in passing to such things as positive welfare rights—rights to subsistence, medical care, a minimum wage, and so forth. They belong to the subject of socioeconomic equality discussed earlier.
42. *Leviathan*, chap. 14.

gets it first or takes it away from the other by force. But exclusive rights, if everyone is to have them, must be designed so that their exercise by one person is not inconsistent with their exercise by another. Hobbes believes that such exclusive rights can arise only through the abandonment by individuals entering civil society of large segments of the nonexclusive rights they possess in the state of nature: The rights of each person that are left standing become exclusive by the abrogation of the natural right by others to interfere with their exercise. Locke, by contrast, regards exclusive rights as natural and pre-societal, notably rights to liberty and property, and he determines their scope essentially as a form of freedom of action which all can exercise without mutual interference.

I would not claim that rights are natural either in Locke's religious sense or in anything near it. But as Hume says, nothing is more natural to human beings than to adopt and uphold the conventions which embody the rights most important for individual security and the survival of society. The recognition of rights is a moral and social practice, but it answers to a need deeply rooted in human nature.

One of the virtues of a system of exclusive rights is that it permits some of the relations between persons to be governed by pure procedural justice. That is, whatever outcome results from the interaction of people who do not violate those rights is regarded as morally acceptable—and since the rights are designed so that they cannot conflict, being essentially degrees of negative freedom which stop when they block the same negative freedom of others, there is always at least one morally acceptable outcome, and usually many.

But this requires that the actual rights be designed so that their consequences will be morally acceptable. A system of pure procedural justice has to be evaluated and justified in terms of its effects on the lives of those living under it. It is not morally primitive. Both the degrees of freedom it protects and the institutional context in which it is embedded must be justified in terms of a range of social and personal values. This is clear if one thinks of property rights, for example, but it applies more widely than that.

I agree for the most part with Scanlon's position in "Rights, Goals, and Fairness," that the explanation or justification of rights, while not simply a matter of utility, should have something in common with rule-utilitarianism in that the moral consequences of the practice as a whole, rather than just the character of an individual act or breach, must be taken into account in determining the scope of the right. These consequences include values other than utility-maximization, and the protection of individuality is important among them. I think there are some deontological restrictions on how people may treat one another that do not rest on such a rule-consequentialist foundation, but they are more important in individual morality than in the justification of rights recognized by the state.[43]

If we think of these guarantees as deriving from the requirements of legitimacy—that is, unanimous acceptability of the basic framework by typically divided individuals—then it is clear that equal importance must be assigned to rights against the coercive power of the state itself and to state enforcement of rights against interference by other people. The standard way to tailor such guarantees involves a specified type of freedom or entitlement together with restrictions of the grounds on which it may permissibly be limited.

Other values besides the protected autonomy or individuality itself influence the design of such practices, and clearly some rights are to an important extent instrumental in their justification. The precise form of property rights, contract, or rights of inheritance should depend substantially on their economic effects over the long run, in respect of both production and distribution, as well as on considerations of liberty. Rights to freedom of expression are strongly supported by their consequences for political accountability and the growth of knowledge, as well as by considerations of individual autonomy. But

43. See *The View From Nowhere*, chap. 9.

some rights, against interference in private conduct, depend much more on the nature of individual human life, and the importance of preserving for each person a private area in which he can lead it and develop his personal relations with other individuals and his own conception of how to live.

The justification for such protections depends, in my view, on the nonaggregative, unanimity-seeking conception of legitimacy. A legitimate social order has to be acceptable, not only from a completely detached perspective, but also to each individual from a mixed perspective which includes recognition of similar mixtures in others. This requires certain strict limits on what may be done to any individual by the potentially vast power of the state, in the service of the general welfare, equality, or perfectionist aims. There is also, as with distributive justice, a strong presumption of negative responsibility on the part of the state for violations which it does not impose but avoidably fails to prevent. That the state is obliged to prevent its citizens from violating one another's rights is not controversial—but its positive responsibility not to violate them itself is even stronger, and in some cases this may override the claims of negative responsibility to rule out policies which, if adopted, would diminish the overall quantity of rights violations.

In deciding what has to be protected in order to preserve the acceptability of the authority of the state, one has to think in general terms about the categories of individual choice and commitment which are important to people, rather than about the particular choices they will make. We are looking for limits which cannot reasonably be rejected by anyone who honestly tries to accommodate everyone's else's point of view. And it is clear that the freedom to arrange one's personal and family life, to develop one's own goals, and to pursue happiness and understanding by one's own lights, has an importance for almost every individual that can hardly be exaggerated. Perhaps the recognition of this can occasionally be beaten out of people, and perhaps some may choose voluntarily to subordinate their individuality to an external authority, but even so, we cannot expect a society to gain the voluntary allegiance of a varied collection of normal human beings unless it accommodates the demand for some personal space in which to maneuver, and treats this not merely as a good to be promoted but as a necessity to be guaranteed for each individual.

That is why the value assigned to the protection of such rights is, to use the technical term, nonaggregative. We have to guarantee the same degree of protection to everyone, rather than increasing the the aggregate amount for all persons if that can be done by giving more to some and less to others. The guarantee of certain forms of inviolability is a straightforward condition of the legitimacy of a political system because anyone who does not enjoy those guarantees could reasonably reject its authority. Aggregative value, on the other hand, can be assigned to benefits if the usual combination of personal and impersonal motives would make it unreasonable to insist on such a guarantee, and more reasonable to allow other principles to govern their distribution. One such method is to leave the decision up to a combination of individual choice and democratic politics—conceived as a mechanism for the aggregation of popular preferences. But the legitimacy of majority rule, and its scope of operation, must be based on a foundation of unanimity.

There are certainly many types of goods for which such tradeoffs are reasonable, but the precise boundaries between the aggregative and the nonaggregative are a matter of dispute. On one side, as I have said earlier, there is a case for raising certain forms of basic public provision—health care, housing, adequate nourishment, education—to the status of rights along with the forms of freedom and inviolability which more usually occupy that position. On the other side, there are still people who would favor protecting economic freedom against encroachment just as freedom of speech or religion is protected. The objection to this libertarian outlook goes back again to the conditions of political legitimacy. Rights cannot be discovered by pure intuition: They must be justified by their role in making it unreasonable for anyone to reject a system which protects them, and reasonable for some to reject a system which does not. For libertarian property rights, I believe the reverse is true. Many people could reasonably reject a system which prohibited taxation to finance redistribution and public goods; and no one could reasonably reject a system just because it permitted such taxation, since that is simply not an intolerable violation of the domain of personal conduct and interpersonal relations. Taxation is not theft. Theft violates legitimate individual expectations based on the institution of property. But there is no legitimate expectation in advance that a society's system of property will include no restrictions on voluntary exchanges or transfers, or minimal ones. Some system of property rights has an indispensable role in the definition of a protected sphere of personal liberty, but that is not it.

Another issue is that of the priority among nonaggregative values, when a society's efforts to secure them threaten to interfere with one another. For example, freedom of expression can be defined more or less broadly. It is standardly limited to exclude incitement to physical harm, or libel. But there is controversy over whether it should also be limited by considerations of group defamation, which are sometimes offered to support restrictions of racist, sexist, or religiously biased expression. (Laws of this kind exist in Western Europe.) While the self-esteem and sense of public respect whose protection motivates such proposals are clearly worthy of some form of effective institutional support, my own opinion is that considerably more harm than good results from conferring on the state the power to restrict expression for such reasons.

There is some psychological contingency in all this. It is conceivable that a population of human beings could exist for whom some collective good was so overwhelmingly important that in its service, a radical curtailment of their individual liberty would be acceptable to each of them, so that their rights could legitimately contract. Something like this happens in wartime, when liberties are curtailed and great sacrifices required to resist the transcendent evil of defeat, and possible massacre. But apart from that, the overwhelming dominance of collective values in the motivation of the members of a society seems rare, and the imposition of those values at great cost in individual freedom does not tend to produce it. Rather it results in the familiar hypocrisy of closed societies and the branding of recalcitrant individuals with ordinary motives as enemies of the people.

Unanimous acceptability of the framework of government can be seriously sought only through the recognition that general unanimity in aims and values does not exist. The only unanimity that makes sense must be based on a combination of such impartial and perfectionist values as it is reasonable to expect everyone to share, together with respect for those large differences in value and conception of life that inevitably remain. This requires agreement on how those differences will and will not be permitted to influence both political choice and individual choice.

The most important rights, of course, are those against being murdered, tortured, or enslaved, followed closely by the rights embodied in due process of law and the politically essential rights of free expression, association, and organization. But the necessity of these is so obvious, in spite of their widespread violation, that I won't rehearse the arguments for them here. (They can be defended on rule-utilitarian as well as on Kantian grounds.) Instead I shall take up, mostly in the next chapter, the broader requirements of toleration which are implied by the principle of legitimacy. The requirements I have in mind place limits on the ways in which the interests of the majority, or the majority's convictions about the interests of everyone, may be advanced even in a democracy by political means.

For example, one of the ways in which this sort of limitation comes under strong pressure in pluralistic societies is through the desire to use the power of the state to control the cultural environment by eliminating what is offensive to the majority, a point emphasized by Ronald Dworkin in his discussion of curbs on sexual freedom.[44] Since sex is one of the most personal ele-

44. See *What Is Equality?* Part III.

ments of life, and one of its most powerful motives, the potential conflict between personal and collective desires is very great here. The recent strong reaction by socially conservative forces in the United States to the sexual liberation of the 1960s and 1970s is a striking example. There is renewed hostility to homosexuals, and to pornography. Such feelings also play a part in the opposition to the right to abortion, which is closely connected with the opposition to sexual freedom, particularly the sexual freedom of women.

While I do not sympathize with the ideals behind this moral environmentalism, it must be recognized that given their values the conservatives do have a genuine interest here, since extensive individual liberty in sexual matters creates an emotional and cultural climate in which their preferred forms of sexual life are more difficult to maintain and to inculcate in their children. (Something similar is true with respect to the economic effects of free enterprise on those who would prefer to live in a simpler, less materialistic culture.) So a choice must be made; not everyone can have what he wants.

I do not think this issue can be settled just by arguing about whose values are the right ones. Pluralism in sexual mores is inevitable, and no single standard can hope to satisfy the condition of unanimous non-rejectability which would be required to legitimate its inclusion among the basic values of a society. The question is whether this means that the matter should be turned over to majoritarian politics, for the aggregation of preferences, or whether the sexual freedom of individuals should be protected from such control by acquiring the status of a right.

It seems to me that the argument for a liberal solution, which gives the second answer, has to depend on the judgment that it is terrible to have one's desired form of sexual expression restricted by others who find it repellent, as part of their own strong sexual feelings. The suppression of homosexuality is so much worse for the homosexual than is the relaxation of ambient taboos and restrictions for the sexual puritan, that even the puritan should decide in favor of freedom unless he is prepared to claim that no legitimate state need consider the potential objections of homosexuals because homosexuality is wicked and worthy of suppression for its own sake. This, however, is not a position that no one could reasonably reject, and the puritan is simply mistaken if he thinks it is. Without such backing, he cannot simply discount as a basis for reasonable rejection the great and evident personal cost to the homosexual of a policy of repression; and he has nothing of comparable weight in his own life to oppose to it as a basis for rejecting a policy of toleration. His deep conviction about how *others* should live cannot make it reasonable for him to advance his values at the cost of their great unhappiness.

If, as we must in a pluralist society, we regard it as a matter of conflicting interests resulting from opposed values which the society simply has to try to contain and accommodate, the issue of sexual inclination is not like the issue between smokers and nonsmokers. For those threatened with repression, it is a matter of the form of their deepest and most acutely personal desires. The freedom to act on those desires is therefore a leading candidate for protection as a right. This does not exclude prohibitions against acute and direct offense to the equally deep sensibilities of others; but it does mean that personal and private activities (including the consumption of pornography) should be protected from political control.

In the United States, these sexual issues have taken up the role which religious controversies would overtly play in American politics if they were not constitutionally excluded from doing so. In both cases, I believe, the requirement to protect individuals from being flattened by the will of the majority depends on similar conditions of legitimacy. In the next chapter I shall take up the issue of toleration, particularly religious toleration, in more detail.

There is a further feature of some rights which deserves comment, and to which I have already alluded in connection with the distinction between positive and negative responsibility. Rights protect the individual against having certain things done to him to produce a greater overall balance of societal good; that is understandable enough as a condition of legitimacy. What seems paradoxical is that, taken strictly, certain rights may not be violated even as a means to the prevention of a larger number of violations of the very same right. There are certain things, such as killing innocent people, which the state ought never to be authorized to do to anyone in the name of its citizens, even in order to prevent worse evils of the same kind. And the state ought to be constrained against using the third degree on suspected criminals, even if this would reduce the frequency of ordinary criminal assault by a more than compensating factor. This is true of certain features of individual morality as well: One may not commit murder to prevent five other murders; torture one innocent person to prevent five others from being tortured, and so forth. Positive responsibility dominates negative responsibility in these cases.

Of course consequentialist arguments can be given in support of such restrictions, but there is another factor as well, which has been pointed out by Frances Myrna Kamm.[45] Such rules, by which murder and torture are *always* wrong, confer a certain status on persons which they do not have in a moral or legal system in which murder and torture are regarded merely as great evils—so that sometimes it may be permissible to commit them in order to prevent even more of the same. Faced with the question whether to murder one to save five from murder, one may be convinced that fewer people will be murdered if one does it; but one would thereby be accepting the principle that anyone is legitimately murderable, given the right circumstances. This is a subtle but definite alteration for the worse in *everyone's* moral status. Whereas if one refuses, one is saying that all murders are illegitimate, including of course the five that one will have refused to prevent.

To preserve the status of every person as someone that it is never legitimate to murder may seem inadequate compensation

---

45. See "Harming Some to Save Others" and *Morality, Mortality*.

for a larger number of murders. But if I may be permitted a somewhat incoherent thought experiment: If I were given a choice between a significant increase in the likelihood of being murdered and the abolition of my moral or legal right not to be murdered, I would choose the former. Somehow that status, abstract as it is, is vitally important, and its recognition by a society is an enormous good in itself, apart from its consequences. More would have to be said to make sense of this intuitive idea, but at the moment I don't know what it is.

I have attempted only to sketch in general terms what rights are and how they are best justified—as a societal guarantee of minimal conditions of personal freedom against the state and against the interference of other persons, needed to make the otherwise enormous extent of state power tolerable to everyone. This depends on the institutional protection of rights, but the institutions themselves must be upheld by people who regard these values as beyond compromise. I now want to say a bit about this psychological dimension of the subject, and about its importance as a safeguard against the dangers of another very powerful psychological element of civilization.

Political theory has always been concerned to design systems which generate the psychological conditions of their own stability, and the search for conditions of legitimacy is an important part of this. But illegitimate systems can also be stable, given a suitable distribution of power, and that raises a major problem which is exacerbated by the successes of political stability and the increasing socialization of human beings.

It is clear that the power of complex modern states depends on the deeply ingrained tendency of most of their members to follow the rules, obey the laws, and do what is expected of them by the established authorities without deciding case by case whether they agree with what is being done. We turn ourselves easily into instruments of higher-order processes; the complex organizational hierarchies typical of modern life could not function otherwise—not only armies, but all bureaucratic institutions rely on such psychological dispositions.

This gives rise to what can be called the German problem. The generally valuable tendency to conform, not to break ranks conspicuously, not to attract attention to oneself, and to do one's job and obey official instructions without substituting one's own personal judgment can be put to the service of monstrous ends, and can maintain in power the most appalling regimes. The same procedural correctness that inhibits people from taking bribes may also turn them into obedient participants in well-organized official policies of segregation, deportation, and genocidal extermination. The problem is whether it is possible to have the benefits of conformity and bureaucratic obedience without the dangers.

The first response will be that these dangers cannot arise in a liberal democracy, so the solution lies at the political level— the methods of political decision must be so designed that a monstrous dictatorship cannot gain control of a complex and highly disciplined modern state. Provided policies are subject to constant popular review and open challenge by the press and democratically elected political representatives, there is no danger in even the most deeply ingrained habit of mindless conformity to orders by those charged with carrying them out.

But this is an exaggeration. Even democratic states can perpetrate horrible crimes, both foreign and domestic; in any case, the problem is very real when democracy is overturned, and we know how disastrous it can be if there is nothing to fall back on at that point. Much of the structure of the state remains in place in such circumstances, and the general habit of obedience does not disappear, so all the organized power that it confers is placed at the disposal of those who are now at the top of the hierarchy. The willingness to use terror is also very important, but a policy of terror itself relies on conformity, as well as reinforcing it.

The question I want to ask is whether the conception of authority on which social order depends can be modified to take account of these dangers. Here, as in so many issues of political theory, we are looking for an alternative to Hobbes's absolute solution to the problem of political stability. Hobbes was both too pessimistic and too optimistic in the assumptions which led to his absolutist conclusions: too pessimistic in believing that no limited government would be stable enough to prevent civil war; too optimistic in believing that no absolute government could be as bad as anarchy. But the issue here is not that of constitutional limits on state power, but rather that of built-in psychological limits on the reach of political authority through the conformity and docility of individuals who occupy social roles.

I believe that there is something to be done along these lines, and that it consists in the pervasive internalization of the conditions of political legitimacy, such as the protection of the most important individual rights, as part of the sense of political authority to which citizens are trained. If the citizenry of a country and particularly the occupants of official positions at all levels are imbued with a conception of legality which is in part substantive and not merely formal, it may have an effect on what can be carried out by the state apparatus. Of course most of what is legally required depends on the laws that have been passed by constitutionally specified procedures that are content-neutral. The inhibitions I am talking about would be essentially negative, leading to unwillingness to continue blindly to play one's role in the service of policies patently offensive to the miminal conditions of political legitimacy, because they subject some groups or individuals to intolerable persecution or oppression.

This is not the same thing as allowing one's personal preferences or judgment in general to overrule the duties defined by one's social role or official position. Policemen and judges and tax collectors would still be expected to carry out the law whether they agreed with it or not, in almost all cases. The exceptions would depend not on personal inclination or private conscience (a different matter, leading to the different topic of conscientious objection), but on a common set of values widely recognized, of which certain acts of government would be regarded as a betrayal.

I realize that this idea has its dangers, and that the resistance of diehard segregationists in the American South during the 1950s and 1960s to the legal enforcement of racial integration would have been defended by them on the basis of such "common values." But my position is not merely formal: I do not suggest that just any widely shared values should place this kind of limit on the authority of government to command the conformity of citizens. Rather, I mean that some of the specific conditions of legitimacy for which I have argued should be embodied not only in a constitution which is itself part of the law, but at least partly in the conditions of willingness to obey without which law cannot exist.

Indeed, in some cases the development of such a mental constitution may run ahead of the strictly legal variety, and through the growing reluctance of individuals to play a role in the enforcement of repugnant laws, may ease the way to their eventual abolition. The extraordinary power of civil disobedience motivated in this way was demonstrated, while this book was being written, by the events of 1989 in Eastern Europe. The pure idea of human rights, kept alive by communities of dissidents, produced a gradual erosion of the authority of Communist governments which had proceeded to the point where withdrawal of Soviet military backing resulted in their swift collapse. The power of universal values, and the vulnerability of governments to loss of moral authority, are the great and hopeful lessons of that extraordinary upheaval.

For this reason the maintenance of the conception of an international standard of human rights, against which all governments should be measured, is of great political importance. It is not just an exercise in moral condemnation of what we are largely powerless to change, but a challenge to the legitimacy of those governmental policies which violate human rights; and in the long run it can contribute to the weakening of the authority of those many governments which persist in such policies. The process is always dangerous and often tragic: The citizens of those countries, if they express doubts about the legitimacy of what is done or fail to conform or to obey orders, face the possibility and often the certainty of terrible consequences. For us lucky ones it is not a very comfortable role to stand safely on the sidelines in a free country loudly offering moral support while others risk their lives. Nevertheless moral support is a genuine and essential form of support, for the sense that one is basing the rejection of governmental authority on a widely recognized standard of decency is extremely important for those who are isolated and weak. For those who make such a choice, moral support is the least we owe them.

14

Toleration

The most intellectually difficult problem regarding an acceptable partition of motives arises not from conflicts of interest but from conflicts over what is truly valuable. Members of a society all motivated by an impartial regard for one another will be led into conflict by that very motive if they disagree about what the good life consists in, hence what they should want impartially for everyone.

Anyone with a particular conviction about the good for human beings will naturally be inclined to get the power of the state behind it, not only for his own sake but out of concern for others. Those who disagree will want the state to promote other ends. Such disagreements can be much more bitter and intractable than mere conflicts of interest, and the question is whether there is any method of handling them at a higher level which all reasonable persons ought to accept, so that they cannot object to the particular result even if it goes against them. Simple impartiality will not generate a solution, since the conflicting positions already embody it, and the difference is over what it means.

Some of these disagreements can be handled within the ordinary life of politics, where arguments over ends are part of the process of gaining majority support for particular policies. But there are other disagreements so deep and so acute that it is not possible to devise a method of fighting them out politically whose results could command the reasonable acceptance of the losers. Conspicuous among them are religious differences, but other convictions about the ultimate meaning of life or the sources of its value should be included as well. For this type of case another device is needed to ensure legitimacy—the exclusion of certain values from the admissible grounds for the application of coercive state power. We must agree to refrain from limiting people's liberty by state action in the name of values that are deeply inadmissible in a certain way from their point of view. This adds something to the purely instrumental theory of toleration. I would like to begin by discussing the principle in rather abstract terms, leaving the consideration of specific policies till later.

What I shall call liberal toleration, using "liberal" in its American sense, depends on the acceptance of an impartiality of a higher order than that which leads us to recognize the equal value of everyone's life. Impartiality among persons could take its content from a specific conception of the good, which others might not share. But the higher-order impartiality I am thinking of operates precisely on the conflicts between different first-order impartialities informed by conflicting conceptions of the good. Opposed ideas of the good, and therefore of what is impartially desirable for everyone—and not only opposed personal interests—are counted among the conflicts with which a legitimate political system must deal, and with respect to which it must try to be fair among its citizens. The opposite view is that in political justification one must rely on one's convictions about what human good consists in, even if it is nothing but the satisfaction of individual preferences—and that it is enough to see that the system treats people impartially with respect to that good, whatever it is.

The intellectual problem is how to make sense of a supposed higher-order impartiality, either logically or morally. It seems to require us to subordinate our concern for people's good to something else, but it is obscure both what that is and why it should carry such weight. Haven't we gone as far as necessary (and perhaps even as far as possible) in taking up other people's point of view when we have accepted the impartial component of our own moral position? The motive for higher-order impartiality is far more obscure than the motive for wanting everyone to have a good life.

It is so obscure that critics of the liberal position on toleration often doubt that its professions of impartiality are made in good faith. Part of the problem is that liberals ask of everyone a certain restraint in calling for the use of state power to further specific, controversial moral or religious conceptions—but the results of that restraint appear with suspicious frequency to favor precisely the controversial moral conceptions that liberals usually hold.

For example, those who argue against the restriction of pornography or homosexuality or contraception on the ground that the state should not attempt to enforce contested personal standards of morality often don't think there is anything wrong with pornography, homosexuality, or contraception. They would be against such restrictions even if they believed it *was* the state's business to enforce personal morality, or if they believed that the state could legitimately be asked to prohibit anything simply on the ground that it was wrong.

More generally, defenders of strong toleration tend to place a high value on individual freedom, and limitations on state interference based on a higher-order impartiality among values tends to promote the individual freedom to which they are partial. This leads to the suspicion that the escalation to a higher level of impartiality is a sham, and that all the pleas for toleration and restraint really disguise a campaign to put the state behind a secular, individualistic, and libertine morality—against religion and in favor of sex, roughly.

Yet liberalism purports to be a view that justifies religious toleration not only to religious skeptics but to the devout, and sexual toleration not only to libertines but to those who believe extramarital sex is sinful. It distinguishes between the values a person can appeal to in conducting his own life and those he can appeal to in justifying the exercise of political power. What I want to know is whether a position of this type is coherent and defensible.

The question is important even though this is only one of the arguments for toleration. A historically significant and politically more effective argument is that those who have the upper hand now may not hold it forever, and that out of prudence they should refrain from imposing a sectarian view on others in exchange for the assurance that they will be treated with similar restraint if they find themselves in the minority. This is an argument for political toleration and impartiality as a second-best solution, acceptable because the best solution—political imposition of your own world view without any risk of future suppression—is not available. Such a defense of toleration as a modus vivendi can be offered to holders of radically divergent moral and religious positions, but it is an instrumental argument, and does not present higher-order impartiality in the political sphere as a value in itself. It could not therefore be offered as a reason for toleration to those who felt certain that their domination of the society was completely secure.

Another argument for toleration would be simply to deny the truth of those religious and moral beliefs which seem to generate reasons against it—acknowledging that we are faced with a battle between world views, which must be fought out at ground level. But apart from the politically suicidal aspect of an attempt to defend toleration by attacking religion, this position fails to account for the *reach* of the argument that many political liberals wish to offer.

Liberal toleration is not compatible with absolutely any set of particular values and beliefs, but there is a version of it which aspires to be acceptable to those who disagree deeply over many other matters of the first importance—including the value of individual autonomy. Even if he cannot convince all of those people, it is important to a liberal of this stripe that he should at least be able to convince *himself* that they have reason to accept certain principles of political toleration and impartiality—and that such acceptance would not require them to abandon their religious or moral views, because his principles don't rest on the denial of those views. This would satisfy the condition of legitimacy as an ideal of possible unanimity at some sufficiently high level with respect to the way disagreements are handled. So my aim is to achieve a certain peace of mind. But I have to say that although I shall offer an answer to the problem of interpretation and justification that has been posed, the unanimity being sought at a higher level is in this case even more doubtful than usual.

To restate the apparent paradox: Liberalism asks that citizens accept a certain restraint in calling on the power of the state to enforce some of their most deeply held convictions against others who do not accept them, and holds that the legitimate exercise of political power must be justified on more restricted grounds—grounds which belong in some sense to a common or public domain.

But it is not clear why this restricted form of justification should be the standard of political legitimacy at all. To put the argument against: Why should I care what others with whom I disagree think about the grounds on which state power is exercised? Why shouldn't I discount their rejection if it is based on religious or moral or cultural values that I believe to be mistaken? Isn't that being *too* impartial, giving too much authority to those whose values conflict with mine—betraying my own values, in fact?[46] If I believe something, I believe it to be *true*, yet here I am asked to refrain from acting on that belief in deference to beliefs I think are false. It is unclear what possible moral motivation I could have for doing that. Impartiality among persons is one thing, but impartiality among conceptions of the good is quite another. True justice ought to consist of giving everyone the best possible chance of salvation, for example, or of a good life. In other words, we have to start from the values that we ourselves accept in deciding how state power may legitimately be used.

And it might be added, aren't we doing that anyway, if we adopt the liberal standard of impartiality? Not everyone be-

---

46. Robert Frost defined a liberal as someone who couldn't take his own side in an argument.

lieves that political legitimacy depends on this condition, and if we impose political institutions on others in our society because they do meet it (and block the imposition of institutions that do not), why aren't we being just as partial to our own values as someone who imposes a state religion? It has to be explained why this is a form of impartiality at all.

To answer these questions we have to identify the moral conception involved and see whether it has the authority to override those more particular moral conceptions that divide us— and if so, to what extent or in what respects. Rawls has said that if liberalism had to depend on a commitment to comprehensive moral ideals of autonomy and individuality, it would become just "another sectarian doctrine."[47] The question is whether its claim to be something else has any foundation.

I believe that underlying the constraints of liberal toleration is the Kantian requirement of unanimity, which I have invoked throughout, usually referring to the first formulation of the categorical imperative, in terms of universalizability. Here I wish to emphasize the second formulation: that one should treat humanity never merely as a means, but always also as an end. On one reading of this principle, it implies that if you force someone to serve an end that he cannot be given adequate reason to share, you are treating him as a mere means—even if the end is his own good, as you see it but he doesn't.[48] In view of the coercive character of the state, the requirement becomes a condition of political legitimacy.

The problem is to interpret it, so that it rules out neither too much nor too little. The position I want to defend depends on a four-fold classification of grounds for coercion: (1) grounds which the victim would acknowledge as valid; (2) grounds which the victim does not acknowledge, but which are nevertheless admissible because he is grossly unreasonable or irrational not

47. "Justice as Fairness: Political not Metaphysical," p. 246.

48. *Foundations of the Metaphysics of Morals,* pp. 429–30. See Onora O'Neill, "Between Consenting Adults," pp. 261–63; and Christine M. Korsgaard, "The Right to Lie: Kant on Dealing with Evil," pp. 330–34.

to acknowledge them; (3) grounds which the victim does not acknowledge, without being irrational, but which are admissible under a higher-order principle which he does acknowledge, or would be unreasonable not to; and (4) grounds which the victim does not acknowledge—either reasonably or even somewhat unreasonably—and which are such that he cannot be required to accept a higher-order principle admitting them into political justification even if most others disagree with him.

It is type (4) that determines the extent of toleration essential to a legitimate system, and the problem is to explain why its supposed instances do not fall under (2) or (3) instead.

To illustrate: Type (1) is exemplified by Hobbesian coercion, where each of us wants to be forced to do something as part of a practice whereby everyone else is forced to do the same, with results that benefit us all in a way that would not be possible unless we could be assured of widespread compliance. This is not really forcing people to do what they don't want to do, but rather enabling them to do what they want to do by forcing them to do it.

Type (2) is exemplified by the enforcement of criminal law against the willfully antisocial, and also by very basic forms of paternalism. In both cases lack of concern about the harms being prevented is unreasonable or irrational. Someone forcibly prevented from committing armed robbery or from drinking lye during a psychotic episode is not being coerced on grounds that he cannot be given sufficient reason to share: He just doesn't recognize their sufficiency.

Type (3) is exemplified by public policies based on judgments over which reasonable persons can disagree, but where it is also reasonable to agree to allow policy to be determined by a political process in which opposing points of view are represented, and given the chance to prevail. Many disagreements over what is good and bad fall into this category, including most of the values and the priorities among them that enter into debates about economic policy, criminal law, and other matters.

Type (4), if it exists, is exemplified most clearly by the political enforcement of religious, sexual, or cultural orthodoxy. The liberal case for toleration depends on showing that such grounds for state coercion cannot be put under either type (2) or type (3), and that they therefore fail the Kantian condition of possible unanimity. This means that they are not just values on which persons who are not grossly unreasonable or irrational may disagree, but values of such a type that a person cannot reasonably be expected to agree to a system which authorizes the use of political power to enforce or promote values opposed to his own, just because the majority accepts them.

This depends on the assumption that one may be justified in holding a belief about something of fundamental importance without having to conclude that those who do not share it are irrational or unreasonable, even though they have been presented with the same reasons or evidence that one has found compelling. It is not easy to say what distinguishes cases like this from others in which the recalcitrance of those who are not convinced can be dismissed as unreasonable. It seems to me clear that as things now are, those who do not accept the truth of a particular religion (or of atheism) ought not to be judged unreasonable by those who do, and that anyone who today is unconvinced by the germ theory of disease must be judged irrational. This is to reject the position that it is reasonable to believe something only on grounds which make it unreasonable or irrational not to believe it. That would make any reasonable belief an adequate ground for coercion, because those who did not accept it after being given those grounds could be coerced on grounds that it was unreasonable for them to reject. Likewise it would be unreasonable to hold any belief that others could reasonably reject and that was therefore not a possible basis for coercion.

I just don't think belief is like that: There is a substantial middle ground between what it is unreasonable to believe and what it is unreasonable not to believe (where belief and nonbelief are taken as exhaustive—so non-belief is not disbelief). Belief is reasonable when grounded on inconclusive evidence plus judgment. In such a case one usually acknowledges the possibility of some further standard to which impersonal appeal can be made, even though it cannot settle existing disagreements at the moment. But even without such a standard, belief may not be unreasonable. In any case, it would be absurd to claim that individuals should decide what to do in their own lives only on grounds which they believe it would be unreasonable for anyone else to reject, including grounds having to do with fundamental values they believe to be objectively correct.

But in the political realm we have to find a more objective form of justification. If those whom we propose to subject to political coercion cannot be expected to accept the values we wish to further by it, we will be justified only if there is another description of the grounds of coercion that they *can* be required to accept. Sometimes, "You lost the election" will serve that purpose, but not always. It depends on whether the issue is one which it is reasonable to require everyone to put to decision by vote.

This is really a problem of how to interpret the familiar role-reversal argument in ethics: "How would you like it if someone did that to you?" That argument invites the further question, "How would I like it if someone did *what* to me?" Since there is more than one true description of every action, the selection of the morally operative one is crucial. If someone believes that by restricting freedom of worship he is saving innocent people from the risks of eternal damnation to which they are exposed by deviation from the true faith, then under *that* description he presumably *would* want others to do the same for him, if he were in spiritual danger. But under the description "restricting freedom of worship," he wouldn't want others to do it to him, since in light of the fact that his is the true faith, this would be to hinder his path to salvation.

For purposes of political argument we have to exclude the description of what is done in the contested terms of a particular faith, and find instead a way of applying the role-reversal argument in terms of descriptions and values that must be accepted by all reasonable parties, as a basis for regulating or handling those disagreements that reason cannot eliminate.

Legitimate government would be impossible if it were never legitimate to impose a policy on those who reasonably rejected the values on which it was based. It is not in general a valid role-reversal argument to ask, "How would you like it if someone did something to you that you reasonably didn't want him to do?" The reply is that you might not like it, but might nevertheless be prepared to accept it, depending on the nature of their reasons and the institutions or procedures under which they were empowered to act on them in opposition to your preferences. The legitimacy of democratic government depends on its ensuring that we can all countenance, even if we don't like, what it may impose on us against our wills. But this means that it is legitimate only if those impositions that we should not be asked to countenance are kept beyond its power.

Why should I not accept the efforts of others, if they can muster the necessary political strength, to ensure my eternal salvation as they understand it by preventing the spread of heresy and atheism? Why is this so different from accepting what I may believe to be deeply misguided policies on public health, national defense, or education, if they are democratically adopted?[49]

The answer here cannot be just in terms of the priority of my interest in basic personal autonomy over other people's interest in promoting what they regard as a desirable moral environment, since we are dealing here not with a conflict of interests but with a conflict over what my most fundamental interests are. Those who wish to limit my religious freedom are doing so, in the case under consideration, with my own best

49. I offered one answer to this question in "Moral Conflict and Political Legitimacy," but while I still believe the conclusion, I no longer think that "epistemological" argument works. I was finally persuaded by arguments that had been urged against me for some time by Lawrence Sager in discussion—arguments also presented by Joseph Raz in "Facing Diversity: The Case of Epistemic Abstinence."

interests in mind.[50] They believe that eternal salvation has priority in any person's good even over basic personal autonomy, and if I shared their views I would have to agree with them. The question is why my conception of my good should block the use of their conflicting conception in the justification of political control over me in this case, but not in others.

I think the problem is that there is no higher-order value of democratic control or pursuit of the good abstractly conceived which is capable of commanding the acceptance by reasonable persons of constraints on the pursuit of their most central aims of self-realization—except for the need to respect this same limit in others. Ethics does not license an unmediated universal altruism, precisely because that leads in ordinary circumstances of disagreement over the nature of the good to inevitable conflict rather than possible unanimity. Mere altruism, surprisingly enough, does not provide a common standpoint from which everyone can reach the same conclusions—and that is the essence of the contractarian or Kantian idea of legitimacy. Altruism by itself generates as many conflicting standpoints as there are conceptions of the good. And where no common standpoint is available at any level to authorize the collective determination by democratic procedures of policies about which individuals find themselves in radical disagreement because of incompatible values, it is best, if possible, to remove those subjects from the reach of political action.

In some cases, such as national defense, a common standpoint can be found despite extreme disagreement, because

50. But in real life one must always be skeptical about this. See John Locke, *A Letter Concerning Toleration:*

> Let them not call in the Magistrate's Authority to the aid of their Eloquence, or Learning; lest, perhaps, whilst they pretend only Love for the Truth, this their intemperate Zeal, breathing nothing but Fire and Sword, betray their Ambition, and shew that what they desire is Temporal Dominion. For it will be very difficult to persuade men of Sense, that he, who with dry Eyes, and satisfaction of mind, can deliver his Brother unto the Executioner, to be burnt alive, does sincerely and heartily concern himself to save that Brother from the Flames of Hell in the World to come. (p. 35)

everyone recognizes that some unified policy is absolutely necessary, and we all have to take the risk that the actual policy decided on will be abhorrent to us. But that is not true of religion and other basic choices regarding what life is about and how it is to be led. There the argument of necessity does not supply a common standpoint capable of containing the centrifugal force of diametrically opposed values, and legitimacy requires that individuals be left free, consistent with the equal freedom of others, to follow their own paths.

We have to answer the question, why this position is not equivalent to the public adoption of an individualistic conception of the good, according to which each person's good consists in his being able to satisfy his preferences or pursue his own freely chosen aims. That of course would be unacceptable to those who hold more unified conceptions: It would be just "another sectarian doctrine," the dread bourgeois individualism, perhaps.

The answer is that the consequences of making such a conception the basis of policy would be quite different from the position of liberal toleration. If a state really set out to promote the good for everyone so interpreted, it would have to try to discourage forms of life that thwarted individual self-expression and inculcated obedience to authority or to divine law, or subordination of personal aims to the collective goals of an organic community. This might argue for restrictions on religious education, for example, or on the formation of private communistic associations. The true liberal position, by contrast, is committed to refusing to use the power of the state to impose paternalistically on its citizens a good life individualistically conceived. Even if one does not like the results, the requirements of legitimacy dominate the desire to benefit others by your own lights, whatever they may be.

The consequences of such a position are complex, for there are several ways in which state action may serve a conception of the good, and they will not all be equally unacceptable to those who do not share it. (1) A state might force people to live in accordance with that conception, or prohibit them from living in ways it condemns. (2) A state might support the realization of the preferred conception, by education or resource allocation, thus involving all citizens and taxpayers indirectly in its service. (3) A state might adopt policies for other reasons which have the effect of making it easier for one conception to be realized than another, thus leading to growth in adherence to the one as opposed to the other.

Clearly the first way is the most illegitimate; examples are restrictions on the free exercise of religion, on the basic style of personal life, or on private sexual conduct. The second is less of an assault on individuals who do not share the dominant values, but still of questionable legitimacy; the clearest example would be public support of an established church. The third is in some degree unavoidable; liberal toleration, for example, though not motivated by the aim of promoting secularism and discouraging religious orthodoxy, may have these effects nevertheless. Hence it will not *be neutral in effect* among conceptions of the good, though it is based on impartiality among those conceptions, and avoids appealing to any of them to justify the use of coercive state power. Impartiality of this kind has to be distinguished from the kind of intrusive even-handedness which would require the use of state power to ensure that the society gives them all an equal chance to flourish.[51]

This therefore is another area in which the distinction between positive and negative responsibility has moral significance with regard to state action. The state is positively responsible for the difficulties of a particular religion if it either suppresses that religion or actively supports another. Citizens who adhere to the disfavored religion clearly have no reason to authorize such policies. But they do not have similar reasons to refuse acceptance of a system which simply fails to prevent the decline of their religious community. There is much more to

51. This point is made by John Rawls in "The Priority of Right and Ideas of the Good."

be said about all this. For example there may be cases of state action not intentionally aimed against a particular community of conviction which nevertheless foreseeably damages it to such an extent and so directly that positive responsibility must be acknowledged, and the action's legitimacy rendered doubtful. But I have attempted only a rough sketch of the liberal position here.

Let me make a further comment about the positive-negative responsibility distinction. The denial of the moral import of that distinction in evaluating a society's policies of taxation and distribution played a significant role in the discussion of socioeconomic equality. Here, by contrast, it has been invoked as relevant to the difference between state support for a religion and other types of impact of state action on the success of a religion. The reason is that the role of the state as actor on behalf of its citizens assumes prominence when the action is based on commitment to values in direct contradiction to the deepest convictions of some citizens about the meaning of life. That, I think, is deeply offensive and unacceptable, and forfeits the state's claim to represent them in a way in which the promotion of other values some of them do not share does not. The objections to it do not apply to the promotion of controversial aesthetic values, for example.

There are also other cases where positive responsibility is particularly important, some of which were discussed in the previous chapter. How the state treats people in its police function should also be constrained by the fact that it is acting in the name of its citizens, and there are things it should not do because there are things they should not do. The constraints of personal morality, which prohibit certain forms of direct harm to others, even as a means to valuable ends, apply in this way to the state as well as to individuals, and the distinction between positive and negative responsibility for such harm applies here. The state also has a stronger negative responsibility for the failure to prevent such harms than individuals have. But this does not obliterate the positive-negative distinction. As was noted earlier, a state is not justified in employing brutal treatment of criminal suspects to fight crime, just because the overall number of brutal acts would be reduced thereby.

To return to the subject of toleration: There remains the question how much disagreement and of what kind the principle of higher-order unanimity can contain. How effectively can the desire to find a common standpoint of justification curb the desire to pursue the transcendent good as one understands it? After all, if someone is willing to commit his own life to a particular conception, and convinced that the alternative is catastrophic, then it may be hard to resist imposing his opinion on others who, understandably but erroneously, fail to accept it. This tendency may be reinforced by the inclination to find them irrational, and thus subject to paternalistic coercion even under the liberal standard. But even without this, it may be difficult to subordinate a concern for their good as he sees it to a requirement of Kantian respect, if he is really convinced that Kantian respect will allow them to doom themselves.

Such a conflict may bring the commitment to legitimacy to the breaking point, but in that respect toleration is not different from other questions of political theory. There are some conceptions of the good and of morality which are incompatible with the ideal of reasonable unanimity that is the heart of the Kantian position. The most one can hope is that it will be able to contain most of the disagreement that divides democratic societies, and that the forms of fanaticism which it cannot accommodate will gradually die out.

15

Limits: The World

It is a consequence of the account of political legitimacy I have proposed that legitimate government will not always be possible. The reasons for this were indicated in a preliminary way in Chapter 5. If fundamental interests or values are too radically opposed it may be impossible to find enough common impartial motivation to support a framework within which all reasonable parties must agree they should be resolved. It may still be possible to call on their self-interest to support an uneasy truce in preference to all-out war. But that will not show that the parties can agree that this is the *right* outcome: rather each side might reasonably reject accommodation if it could win the conflict outright, but be willing to accept a modus vivendi as the second-best solution if the only real alternative is still worse.

One cause of this situation is the conflict between systems of value so opposed that the adherents of each not only think the other completely wrong, but they cannot accord the others freedom to act on their values without betraying their own. The issue of abortion may have this character: Some people may be unable to accept the legitimacy of a system which prohibits it, and others may be unable to accept the legitimacy of a system which permits it. Another example may be the original conflict between Jews and Arabs over the creation of Israel as a Jewish state with the law of return. Some disagreements, in other words, can make agreement on conditions of justice for their resolution impossible: Nothing the parties are constrained by reason to agree on would have the necessary weight, and they are

thrown back on the attempt to impose their own point of view
by the means available. Admittedly, such conflicts will usually
be attributed by each party to an unreasonable conviction or
demand by the other, and sometimes one of them will be right;
but the gap cannot always be closed in this way.

The problem is most serious when the conflicting values or
convictions have direct implications for the basic conditions of
a just political order. Justice may enable parties to adjudicate
their differences of interest and some of their differences in
conception of the good, but it cannot regulate their differences
about justice. To live together peacefully in such circumstances
they will have to find some still higher-order moral or at any
rate practical idea.

The world as a whole contains cultural and national communities representing such radically diverse values that no conception of a legitimate political order can be constructed under
which they could all live—a system of law backed by force that
was in its basic structure acceptable to them all. Unfortunately
this can also happen within the boundaries of a single state; but
in the world as a whole the diversity is extreme. That is one
reason why a legitimate government of the world is not possible. So long as the world is as divided as it now is, by religious
and cultural xenophobia, the situation will not change.

But there is another reason, more theoretically troubling but
I think equally real, a reason having to do not with the radical
conflict of fundamental values, but with the extreme character
of the conflict of universal interests. I mean the enormous gap
between rich and poor. Inequality can be so extreme that it
makes a legitimate solution unattainable, except possibly over a
long period by gradual stages each of which lacks legitimacy,
or (improbably) over a shorter period by a cataclysmic revolution which also lacks legitimacy.

This problem too can exist within the boundaries of a state,
and in fact some poor countries such as India and Mexico have
wealthy minorities; but it is most spectacular internationally, as
we are constantly being reminded. The distance in standard of

living between the industrialized democracies and the under-
developed countries is staggering despite its familiarity, and those
born into a subsistence economy or worse are the victims of
incredibly bad luck. No one could say that such a situation is
generally acceptable at any level. But I believe that there is also
no alternative available in the short run which it would be unreasonable for anyone to reject, on the basis of a plausible mixture of personal and impersonal motives.

That does not mean improvements are not possible. It only
means that every change will lead to a situation in which someone still has a legitimate complaint. In a system of radical inequality, change can be either gradual or revolutionary: intro-
ducing a modest level of relief for the poor, at moderate cost
to the rich, or expropriating the rich completely for the benefit
of the poor. Forget for the moment how these things would be
accomplished, or whether they could be; the question is, should
either of them be accepted by all parties insofar as they are
reasonable? I believe not. In cases of extreme inequality the
poor can refuse to accept a policy of gradual change and the
rich can refuse to accept a policy of revolutionary change, and
neither of them is being unreasonable in this. The difference
for each of the parties between the two alternatives is just too
great.

I don't mean that whenever someone has a great deal to lose
from a social arrangement it is reasonable for him to reject it.
Slaveowners have a great deal to lose from the abolition of slavery, but the physical coercion and deprivation of liberty imposed on slaves by slaveowners is such an evil and the advantages of slaveowners depend on it so directly that the impersonal
demand to end it renders irrelevant the personal sacrifice by
slaveholders of those advantages, which should themselves be
found unacceptable. But when it is a matter of the relative economic conditions of most citizens of the United States and
Western Europe versus the peasant populations of China and
India, the situation is different, at least on the plausible assumption that Western wealth is derived primarily from tech-

nological superiority and not from the exploitation of those people or the plunder of their resources, and that the under-development of those countries is not due primarily to Western imposition. The degree of sacrifice by the rich that it would be reasonable for the poor countries to insist on in some hypo-thetical collective arrangement is one which it would not be un-reasonable for the rich to refuse.

In other words, perspective enters into what is reasonable, in ways that can sometimes make reasonable unanimity impossi-ble. Each party is assumed in such a case to be subject to three distinct types of reasons: (a) egalitarian impartiality, (b) per-sonal interests and commitments, and (c) consideration for what can reasonably be asked of others. Together these may fail to pick out any solution on which all reasonable persons must con-verge.

Specifically, the poor may recognize that the rich are not un-reasonable to resist more than a certain level of sacrifice, in light of their constellation of motives, while at the same time the poor may reasonably refuse to accept the resulting degree of benefit as sufficient, even in light of the recognition that the rich can reasonably refuse more. From the point of view of the poor, respect for what it is reasonable to require of the rich is dominated by the immediate urgency of their own needs. Sim-ilarly, the rich can recognize this and take it into account with-out having to conclude that their own resistance is unreason-able. In short, resistance to a reasonable aim may itself be rea-sonable.

It is only when we speak of reasonable *solutions*, or proposals, or requests, that we imply that it would be unreasonable for any party to the issue to reject them. Reasonable persons may however fail to converge on a solution that is reasonable *tout court*, without finding one another unreasonable. The classes of outcomes that it is unreasonable for each of them to reject may not intersect. In the case of the single life jacket, there is no reasonable solution, and neither parent is unreasonable to try to grab it for his child as against the other.

As I conceive it, this does not amount to a moral bias in favor of the status quo, except insofar as losing what one has is harder to accept and therefore somewhat more reasonable to reject than not getting what one doesn't have. I don't believe that that should be a large element in the moral calculation: The main thing is the identification of the feasible alternatives, and the size of the difference a choice among them would make for each of the parties.

One implication of this view that some may find unsatisfactory is that in some circumstances existing equality, and not only existing inequality, might be illegitimate. If a significant segment of a strongly egalitarian society could identify a feasible alternative under which they would be much better off in important ways, while others would be worse off, this might give them a sufficient reason to reject the status quo even though those who benefit from it would be just as reasonable to reject a move to the less equal alternative.[52]

If there is no solution that no one could reasonably reject, neither party to the conflict can be reproached for trying to impose a solution acceptable to him but unacceptable to his opponent. Both the status quo and a revolutionary alternative may meet this condition. The fact that the status quo *is* the status quo usually means that those whom it favors have the power to impose it; but if in such circumstances others acquire the power to overthrow it, they cannot be reproached for using it.

I believe the world contains inequalities so great that they generate this moral situation. To be sure, there are significant

52. Not any possible alternative would do for this purpose: To provide a ground for *reasonable* rejection of the status quo, the alternative would have to depend not on the arbitrary assignment of greater advantages to certain individuals or groups, but on a different balance between the weight of personal and impartial egalitarian claims in the design of social institutions, and a different consequent allocation of the benefits and burdens of social cooperation. (The thought that one could be a hereditary monarch, or that one's profession could be heavily subsidized at public expense, does not establish a feasible alternative by comparison with which it would be reasonable to reject the status quo.)

sacrifices—much greater than those commonly accepted—that it is unreasonable for the rich to refuse for the benefit of the poor; and there are other sacrifices so great that it would be unreasonable of the poor to impose them on the rich, even if they were able to do so. But between these two outer boundaries there is a gap, within which fall all those levels of sacrifice which the poor would have sufficient reason to impose if they could and which the rich have sufficient reason to resist if they can. This may seem to authorize pure selfishness, but that is too harsh a word for resistance to a radical drop in the standard of living of oneself and one's family.

Of course it depends on how well off one is. I emphatically do not believe that the ungenerous present conduct of most developed countries falls within this "not unreasonable" range. Particularly with respect to the very poorest countries, ravaged by malnutrition and easily cured diseases, the cost of aid is ludicrously small in relation to the lives that could be saved and the misery prevented. A move to a minimally decent level of international assistance deserves unanimous political support as an intermediate egalitarian goal, in the same way that the guarantee of a decent social minimum does in the domestic case. But the continued protection of the national economic interest by prosperous countries, subject to a substantial increase of international generosity, is simply a direct expression of the warranted and natural personal motivation of their citizens.[53]

If we put together these two factors—extreme economic inequality and extreme opposition of fundamental values—it is no wonder that the world is not a plausible candidate for a single state. The conditions of reasonable unanimity on terms of cooperation and mechanisms for the adjudication of conflicts of interest and value do not exist. It would be close to the

---

53. At present technology gives the predominance of military power to the industrialized nations, but if that should ever change, then the practical significance of the moral situation here described would be completely reversed. The challenge to world economic inequality, and its defense, may eventually take a form which dwarfs the Cold War in retrospect.

truth to say that if a legitimate world government were possible, it would not be necessary. The narrowing and softening of the divisions in value and interest which would be required before it would be right for everyone to accept the authority of a single government would also make it possible for different nations to live peacefully together under a system of multilateral agreements and loose institutions of cooperation not backed up by a monopoly of force. But until all nations in the world become liberal democracies capable of providing their citizens with a decent standard of living, we will have to think of something else.[54]

The community of nations is not exactly a Hobbesian state of nature, but such law and order as it enjoys cannot claim true moral legitimacy, since it is simply the result of the balance of forces among parties who are in fundamental ways mutually too opposed to arrive at reasonable unanimity. They may find a strong common interest in certain arrangements and some common values, but it is not enough to permit the affirmation of a common standard of what is morally right. So they must be content with something less, in the hope that it will grow to include more in the way of ethical standards eventually.

The development of legitimacy within states has been a slow process, generally beginning from sovereign power exercised without much regard for legitimacy in the sense in which I have been using the term. In many states the process has hardly begun, and the Hobbesian task of ending anarchy and imposing the sword is still under way. It would be dreadful if the world

54. Immanuel Kant envisions such a development:

> [I]f by good fortune one powerful and enlightened nation can form a republic (which is by its nature inclined to seek perpetual peace), this will provide a focal point for federal association among other states. These will join up with the first one, thus securing the freedom of each state in accordance with the idea of international right, and the whole will gradually spread further and further by a series of alliances of this kind.

Perpetual Peace, p. 356; p. 104 in Reiss. For a fascinating historical defense of Kant's prescience, see Michael Doyle, "Kant, Liberal Legacies, and Foreign Affairs."

as a whole had to recapitulate this history, but that would be
the inevitable result if the power of world sovereignty were established first—by conquest, for example. Perhaps instead we
can contemplate the gradual development of a degree of international sovereignty as a consequence rather than as a precon-
dition of the development of a common sense of political right
and wrong.

This means that little can be done at the international level,
except through the gradual encroachment of ideas, about the
horrible injustice that currently exists within many states. In
fact the repugnance which many societies evoke must be overcome to the extent of including them in the international community of agreements and conventions, permitting a thin system of law to govern what it can govern and postponing the
rest to a better age. Even if this is not dressed up with self-
serving rhetoric about each nation's right to control its own internal affairs, it can be accepted as a necessity, in all but the
most unbearable cases. What we have here is not a morally
grounded restraint like that of the state toward personal relations within families, but rather a practical limit on the leverage
of any system of law not based on true legitimacy.

This is an unsatisfactory state of affairs, but there is at the
moment no alternative which would be more satisfactory. A
world legal order must content itself with expressing those values and protecting those interests which are shared by most of
the existing states, many of which are morally abominable. The
affirmation of human rights by international agreements is an
important investment for the long term; but the international
protection of individuals, who are the whole point of morality
and political theory, will inevitably remain rather weak for the
present, and largely dependent on informal pressure.

Even if the world changes greatly for the better over the course
of the next few centuries, there will remain strong reasons against
the unlimited growth of world sovereignty. These derive from
the natural pluralism of humanity, and the desirability of allowing that pluralism to receive political as well as individual

expression. Of course the correspondence between cultural or moral pluralism and the boundaries of political units is at best rough and often nonexistent, so that any legitimate state must take into account and respect the pluralism that exists within it, by enforcing basic individual rights, toleration, and freedom of voluntary association. Still, the historical continuity of certain nations and peoples calls for political expression—expression through the collective choice of laws, policies, and institutions by a process in which they rather than the whole world are the primary participants.

This is not because nations or peoples have in themselves an irreducible right to self-determination, but rather because most individuals are fundamentally identified with such groups, and an essential part of their self-expression as individuals will be thwarted if they cannot take part in the political self-definition and development of the group in which their identity is rooted. It is impossible to ignore this even if one's own feelings of national identification are much weaker than the average, as is often true of cosmopolitan intellectuals. Some nations, like the United States, are unified by a political and commercial culture which encompasses great diversity in other respects; others, nonimmigrant societies with long histories such as Japan or Sweden, are unified at a much deeper level. But in neither case would it make sense to elevate the primary level of political community to a more universal plane.

I say this with some uneasiness, not only because of the terrible things that have been done and continue to be done in the name of national self-expression, but because of the pessimism it reflects about the capacity of human beings to place an impartial regard for humanity ahead of their more particular ethnic identities as a principle of political motivation. But this is just another basic aspect of the personal perspective, and it is not going to disappear.

It brings us, also, to a further reason not to expect or hope for the gradual enlargement of political units, ending with a world government. That is the importance of the constantly invoked factor of solidarity in making political systems work. Solidarity requires identification with those with whom one feels it. For that reason there is always a potentially sinister side to it: It is essentially exclusive. Solidarity with a particular group means lack of identification with, and less sympathy for, those who are not members of that group, and often it means active hostility to outsiders; but to some extent this is inevitable, and it is such a powerful source of political allegiance to institutions which deal equitably with members of the group that it must be relied on.[55] By the same token, its absence will weaken the support for cooperative efforts in certain collectivities, particularly if they contain subgroups whose solidarity is strong. I myself find solidarity which depends on racial, linguistic, or religious identification distasteful, but there is no denying its politically cohesive, and disruptive, power. It makes sense, therefore, to pursue legitimacy primarily at the level of the nation-state or where necessary its subdivisions, whether or not the conditions exist for some sort of just international order.

An observation is appropriate here parallel to one made earlier about the relation between political legitimacy and the morality of individual conduct. The license individuals have to concentrate on their own lives and those they specially care about is morally unproblematic only if they can exercise it in the con-

---

55. Compare Sigmund Freud, *Civilization and its Discontents*, chap. 5:

> It is always possible to bind together a considerable number of people in love, so long as there are other people left over to receive the manifestations of their aggressiveness. . . . In this respect the Jewish people, scattered everywhere, have rendered most useful services to the civilizations of the countries that have been their hosts; but unfortunately all the massacres of the Jews in the Middle Ages did not suffice to make that period more peaceful and secure for their Christian fellows. When once the Apostle Paul had posited universal love between men as the foundation of his Christian community, extreme intolerance on the part of Christendom towards those who remained outside it became the inevitable consequence. . . . Neither was it an unaccountable chance that the dream of Germanic world-dominion called for anti-semitism as its complement; and it is intelligible that the attempt to establish a new, communist civilization in Russia shoud find its psychological support in the persecution of the bourgeois. One only wonders, with concern, what the Soviets will do after they have wiped out their bourgeois. (pp. 114f)

text of a just social order, which gives expression to their more impersonal motives without encroaching unacceptably on the personal domain. Otherwise individualistic morality makes for an uneasy conscience. The same is true of the relation between each state and the world. The collective pursuit of prosperity and justice for themselves by the citizens of a nation remains under a shadow while it goes on in a world like ours, where a minority of nations are islands of relative decency in a sea of tyranny and crushing poverty, and the preservation of a high standard of life depends absolutely on strict controls on immigration. The most universal form of that impersonal concern which I have claimed is a natural element of human motivation is left in that case without effective expression. We will be able to tend our own gardens with a good conscience only when this surrounding situation has improved radically, and international institutions of some kind sustain a world order within which the natural pursuit of national interests forms part of a universally acceptable pattern of international relations, like the pursuit of personal life in a just society.

Bibliography

Beitz, C.
Political Equality. Princeton University Press, 1989.

Bentham, J.
"Outline of a Work Entitled Pauper Management Improved." In John Bowring, ed., *The Works of Jeremy Bentham,* vol. 8. Edinburgh: Wm. Tait, 1843; reprint ed. New York: Russell & Russell, 1962.

Burke, E.
Reflections on the Revolution in France (1790). Edited by J. G. A. Pocock. Indianapolis: Hackett, 1987, pp. 1–218.

Carens, J.
Equality, Moral Incentives, and the Market: An Essay in Utopian Politico-Economic Theory. University of Chicago Press, 1981.

Cohen, J., and Rogers, J.
On Democracy. New York: Penguin Books, 1983.

Crocker, L.
"Equality, Solidarity, and Rawls' Maximin." *Philosophy & Public Affairs* 6 (1977).

Doyle, M.
"Kant, Liberal Legacies, and Foreign Affairs." *Philosophy & Public Affairs* 12 (1983).

Dworkin, R.
"What Is Equality?" Parts I and II. *Philosophy & Public Affairs* 10 (1981).
"What Is Equality?" Part III. *Iowa Law Review* 73 (1987).

Freud, S.
Civilization and Its Discontents (1930). Translated in the *Standard Edition of the Complete Psychological Works of Sigmund Freud,* vol. 21. London: Hogarth, 1961.

Gauthier, D.
Morals by Agreement. Oxford University Press, 1986.

Gibson, M.
  "Rationality." *Philosophy & Public Affairs* 6 (1977).

Hare, R. M.
  Freedom and Reason. Oxford University Press, 1963.

Hobbes, T.
  Leviathan (1651).

Kamm, F.
  "Harming Some to Save Others." *Philosophical Studies* 57 (1989).
  Morality, Mortality. Oxford University Press, forthcoming.

Kant, I.
  Foundations of the Metaphysics of Morals (1785), Prussian Academy
  Edition, vol. 4. Translated by H. J. Paton in *The Moral Law.* London: Hutchinson, 1948.
  *On the Common Saying: "This May Be True in Theory, but It Does Not
  Apply in Practice"* (1793), Prussian Academy Edition, vol. 8. Translated in H. Reiss, ed., *Kant's Political Writings.* Cambridge University Press, 1970.
  Perpetual Peace (1795), Prussian Academy Edition, vol. 8. Translated in H. Reiss, ed., *Kant's Political Writings.* Cambridge University Press, 1970.

Korsgaard, C.
  "The Right to Lie: Kant on Dealing with Evil." *Philosophy & Public
  Affairs* 15 (1986).

Locke, J.
  A Letter Concerning Toleration (1689). Edited by J. H. Tully. Indianapolis: Hackett, 1983, pp. 21–58.

Michelman, F.
  "Foreword: On Protecting the Poor Through the Fourteenth
  Amendment." *Harvard Law Review* 83 (1969).
  "In Pursuit of Constitutional Welfare Rights: One View of Rawls'
  Theory of Justice." *University of Pennsylvania Law Review* 121 (1973).

Mill, J. S.
  Utilitarianism (1861).
  Chapters on Socialism (published posthumously in 1879). In S. Col-
  lini, ed., *On Liberty and Other Writings.* Cambridge University Press,
  1989.

Nagel, T.
  The Possibility of Altruism. Oxford University Press, 1970; reprint
  ed. Princeton University Press, 1978.

"Rawls on Justice," *Philosophical Review* 82 (1973). Reprinted in N. Daniels, ed., *Reading Rawls*. New York: Basic Books, 1975; reprint ed. Stanford University Press, 1989.

Mortal Questions. Cambridge University Press, 1979.

The View From Nowhere. Oxford University Press, 1986.

"Moral Conflict and Political Legitimacy." *Philosophy & Public Affairs* 16 (1987).

Nozick, R.
Anarchy, State, and Utopia. New York: Basic Books, 1974.

O'Neill, O.
"Between Consenting Adults." *Philosophy & Public Affairs* 14 (1985).

Parfit, D.
Reasons and Persons. Oxford University Press, 1984.

On Giving Priority to the Worse Off (unpublished manuscript, 1989).

Rawls, J.
A Theory of Justice. Harvard University Press, 1971.

"Reply to Alexander and Musgrave." *Quarterly Journal of Economics* 88 (1974).

"Justice as Fairness: Political not Metaphysical." *Philosophy & Public Affairs* 14 (1985).

"The Priority of Right and Ideas of the Good." *Philosophy & Public Affairs* 17 (1988).

"Justice as Fairness" (unpublished manuscript presented at New York University, October, 1989).

Raz, J.
"Facing Diversity: The Case of Epistemic Abstinence." *Philosophy & Public Affairs* 19 (1990).

Scanlon, T. M.
"Rawls' Theory of Justice." *University of Pennsylvania Law Review* 121 (1973). Partly reprinted in N. Daniels, ed., *Reading Rawls*. New York: Basic Books, 1975; reprint ed. Stanford University Press, 1989.

"Rights, Goals, and Fairness." In S. Hampshire, ed., *Public and Private Morality*. Cambridge University Press, 1978.

"Contractualism and Utilitarianism." In A. Sen and B. Williams, eds., *Utilitarianism and Beyond*. Cambridge University Press, 1982.

Scheffler, S.
The Rejection of Consequentialism. Oxford University Press, 1982.

Schelling, T.
  Choice and Consequence. Harvard University Press, 1984.

Sen, A.
  "Rational Fools: A Critique of the Behavioral Foundations of Economic Theory." *Philosophy & Public Affairs* 6 (1977).

Wiggins, D.
  "Claims of Need." In *Needs, Values, Truth.* Oxford: Basil Blackwell, 1987.

Index